KT-493-300

PREACHING THROUGH THE CHRISTIAN YEAR

2

PREACHING THROUGH THE CHRISTIAN YEAR

2

Sermon outlines for the Seasons and Holy Days of the Church's year

Frank Colquhoun

MOWBRAYS
LONDON & OXFORD

© A. R. Mowbray & Co Ltd 1972

Printed in Great Britain by
Alden & Mowbray Ltd
at the Alden Press, Oxford

ISBN 0 264 64594 4

First published 1972
by A. R. Mowbray & Co Ltd
The Alden Press, Osney Mead,
Oxford, OX2 0EG

PREFACE

The only claim I would make for these sermon outlines is that they are firmly and quite unashamedly based on the Bible. In putting them together my concern has been to offer some fairly solid scriptural material to those who wish to 'keep festival' and preach within the framework of the Christian year. How the material is actually presented on any occasion will naturally depend upon the preacher's own style and technique as well as upon the make-up of his congregation. I am aware that in some cases the outlines are overloaded. I am also aware that I have been somewhat sparing in the use of illustrations. The wise preacher will draw his illustrations from contemporary life, and from his own experience, rather than from textbooks. The two or three sermons based on hymns, and the allusions to hymns in others, reflect my own interest in hymnody.

F.C.

CONTENTS

Part One. Church Seasons

Part Two. Holy Days

INTRODUCTION

Preaching is unable to stand by itself. Alone it is insufficient to build up the Church's life. Preaching must always operate in a context. It must be buttressed.

Let me illustrate. Here is a congregation with a Chrysostom for a preacher. Spell-binders are rare in the modern Church, but not so completely unimaginable that we cannot at least visualise the situation. Crowds flock in to hear this preacher. Clearly the man in the pulpit has a charisma. Nevertheless if something else is not supplied in that congregation the crowds will as easily flock out, especially when that particular preacher departs.

Not infrequently the above illustration is employed to demonstrate the futility of preaching. What in fact it demonstrates is the weakness of preaching when it is relied upon to accomplish more than it has the capacity to produce. Preaching cannot stand by itself. Those who listen to preaching must be offered more than preaching. They must be offered a structured church life into which they may be incorporated, and this structured life includes the sacraments. Otherwise they will not be rooted, they will not be nourished, and they will not stand.

The name of St Francis is associated with compassion for the poor and with preaching; too often his preoccupation with organising is overlooked. John Wesley almost lives as the image of the preacher, but where would Methodism have been without Wesley's concentration on organising the life of the congregation? The preaching needed the class meetings and the hymns, it was insufficient by itself.

There are two sides to the life of the Church and strikingly enough they are both represented by Whitsunday. Whitsunday marks the coming of the Spirit in the fulness of power, it also represents the birthday of the organised Church. There is always a tension between these two sides, but if the Church neglects either, it does so at its peril.

Preaching belongs to the 'life in the Spirit' side, but if it tries to imagine itself self-sufficient, with an inbuilt capacity to exist independently of any reliance upon organisation in the sense of a structured church life it will fail. At the present time there is an impatience with church structures. Not surprisingly is this so since a disproportionate time seems to have been occupied with them, but they are indispensable; and if preaching gets itself into the position of setting itself over against church structures as belonging to the supposed superior spiritual side of church life it will seriously undermine its own usefulness. The truth is the structures need the Spirit or they are dead, and the life in the Spirit needs the structures or it is evanescent.

The sermon outlines in this book have been written by one known for his work in providing prayers for use in church worship and in church life generally. His interest in this is betrayed in these outlines by his frequent reference to hymns. What he has written, therefore, is for use in the ordinary week-by-week life of the structured Church. These outlines are not star sermons. They are not for star preachers, nor are they outlines for star occasions. The author himself would be the first to admit that they are not literary productions or academic expositions. What he has provided is a series of straightforward biblical sermon outlines, suitable for adaptation to parochial preaching. These sermons could not stand on their own, but they could contribute life to the structured worship of the Church if served with prayer and imaginative handling. This is their justification.

D. W. Cleverley Ford

Part One. Church Seasons

ADVENT

Four judgements

1 Corinthians 4.3, 4 '*With me it is a very small thing that I should be judged by you or by any human court. I do not even judge myself. I am not aware of anything against myself, but I am not thereby acquitted. It is the Lord who judges me.*'

Some ninety years ago Dr James Stalker, an eminent Scottish divine of his day, preached a sermon on this text which he later published under the title of 'The Four Men'. He pointed out that in these words the apostle says that there are four judgements to which he is exposed; first, that of his friends—'judged by you'; secondly, that of the world—'or by any human court'; thirdly, his own judgement—'I do not even judge myself'; and fourthly, God's judgement—'it is the Lord who judges me'.

Dr Stalker remarked that these four judgements reveal man in four different lights; and so he went on to claim that in every man there are in fact four men; the man the world sees, the man as seen by those who know him best, the man as seen by himself, and the man whom God sees.

The important thing that emerges from this is that the verdict passed on a man depends on who his judge is. Paul mentions four such judges. He also tells us what estimate he puts on each of them. Let us consider them for ourselves and see what their opinions are worth.

1. *The judgement of the world*

The apostle says that in exercising his Christian stewardship he is little concerned about what the world thinks of him. 'With me it is a very small thing that I should be judged by any human court.' And in one sense we are bound to agree with him. The judgement the world passes on us as Christians may be of little account. It is bound to be superficial and uninformed and could be far wide of the mark.

Yet let's be clear that this judgement cannot be written off altogether. St Paul himself, in more than one of his letters, insists that those who follow Christ must take care to see that their lives are not a reproach to the world—that is, to those outside the Church. For example, he urges the Christians at Thessalonica not to be idle busybodies but to mind their own affairs and to be hard-working—'so that you may command the respect of outsiders, and be dependent on nobody' (1 Thessalonians 4.12).

In much the same way, when writing to Timothy about the qualifications required of those to be ordained to the office of bishop, the apostle remarks, 'He must have a good reputation with the non-Christian public, so that he may not be exposed to scandal and get caught in the devil's snare' (1 Timothy 3.7, NEB). There is more to the same effect elsewhere in the New Testament. In this sense the world's judgement does matter and cannot be ignored.

2. *The judgement of our friends*

When Paul says to the Corinthians, 'It is a small thing that I should be judged by *you*', he is referring to those *inside* the Church, not to outsiders. He is speaking of the judgement of people who were his friends and knew him well. What is their judgement worth? The apostle asserts that he is little concerned about it. But can we afford to ignore it?

It must be clear that the judgement of our friends counts for more than that of the world. They know a lot more about us. They are able to get a closer view. As a result they may see a very different man from what the world sees. Perhaps they see a better man, for the world may have cruelly misjudged us and formed a quite mistaken verdict. On the other hand our friends may see a worse man; for perhaps we have successfully kept up a false appearance in the eyes of the world but have not been able to deceive those who know us best—especially those in our own family circle.

I knew a man once who was highly thought of in the world. He was a pillar of society, a model churchman, a supporter of charitable causes, and so on. But in his home, as I discovered later, he was tyrannical, close-fisted, bad-tempered, and his children went in fear of him. What passed outside for sanctity was seen nearer at hand as mere hypocrisy.

Those who know us best may not always be our best judges, but it would be stupid to disregard their opinions. If they offer us correction or criticism we would be wise to take heed of it, on the principle that 'faithful are the wounds of a friend'. They know us better than those outside. They may know us better than we know ourselves. In fact, just how well *do* we know ourselves?

Paul faces that question in our text.

3. *The judgement of ourselves*

'I do not judge myself,' he says. And he goes on, 'I am not aware of anything against myself, but I am not thereby acquitted.' He meant that although his conscience was clear, he did not regard that in itself as enough. He was not his own final judge.

This is true for us as well. Yet it is equally true that there is a place in life for self-judgement. The apostle says as much later in this same letter when he warns his readers against 'unworthy' participation in the Lord's supper. 'Let a man examine himself, and so eat of the bread and drink of the cup.' Failure to do this will bring judgement. 'But if we judged ourselves truly, we should not be judged' (1 Corinthians 11.28–31). Our Lord referred to the same thing in his parable of the beam and the moat. In effect what he meant was, judge yourself before you attempt to judge your brother-man.

Do we judge ourselves? We ought to do so; and we are in a better position to do it than others, for we alone can read our hearts and examine our true motives and desires. The fact is, there is a secret world within every man which is known only to himself and it is there he must exercise his judgement.

But there is a higher court still.

4. *The judgement of God*

Having declared that in his stewardship of the gospel he is not ultimately concerned about the judgement of men, the apostle brings his argument to a head by asserting, 'It is the Lord who judges me.' And he adds: 'Therefore do not pronounce judgement before the time, before the Lord comes, who will bring to light the things now hidden in darkness and will disclose the purposes of the heart. Then every man will receive his commendation from God.'

Before the Lord comes. Note that phrase. It is here that the subject of judgement links up with the Advent message. As the collect puts it, the Lord Jesus is coming again in his glorious majesty to judge both the living and the dead. God has committed all judgement to the Son. It is to him we shall have to give our account; and to him all hearts are open, all desires known, and from him no secrets are hid.

Do we believe that? And do we live as though we believed it? If so, it could make an enormous difference to the things we think and say and do. To recognize that we are living daily and hourly, in Milton's words, as in our great Taskmaster's eyes, is to give to life a new seriousness. It is to cease to please men and to seek only to please the Lord. It is to lose the fear of man and to fear God alone. It is to care little for our own reputation and to have a consuming desire for the honour of Christ.

'It is the Lord who judges me.' Let us remember that. We may deceive others. We may deceive ourselves. But we cannot deceive God.

ADVENT

An Advent watchword

I Corinthians 16.22 '*Maranatha*'.

Some of the most popular programmes on the radio and television are concerned with words and their meaning. This is because words are such fascinating things to study. They seem to have an almost inexhaustible interest; and the more we examine them the more we realise how limited is our knowledge of the English language.

I have a word for you today which, if used in a Bible quiz, would probably baffle most Christians. It's an unusual word and is found only once in the New Testament. It comes rather abruptly at the end of the first letter to the Corinthians, after a stern warning to those who do not love our Lord. Suddenly, as if to relieve his feelings, St Paul writes, *Maranatha*! Yes, that's the word. *Maranatha*!

You may well say, 'What in the world does it mean? It's Greek to me!' In actual fact the word is not Greek but Aramaic —and that in itself is significant. It tells us something about the origin of the word. For Aramaic was the language spoken by the Jews in Palestine and we may be sure therefore that this Aramaic word comes from the early Palestinian Church. It is a genuinely primitive word. It belongs to the very beginnings of Christianity. What does it mean?

1. *The Lord and his coming*

Scholars are not altogether certain how to translate this Aramaic expression. But at least it is clear that the word is made up of two parts, *Maran* and *atha*, and that these two parts are concerned with our Lord and with his coming. What is not so clear is whether the verb is an indicative or an imperative. If it is an indicative it states a fact and means 'Our Lord has come' or 'Our Lord is present'.

But while that makes perfectly good sense, it is now thought that the phrase is an imperative and voices a prayer—'Our Lord, come!' This in fact is how it is rendered in the RSV and the NEB. It echoes the prayer with which the book of Revelation finishes: 'He who testifies to these things says, "Surely I am coming soon." Amen. Come, Lord Jesus!'

If this, as it seems, is the correct rendering of *Maranatha*, then it has to do with our Lord's second coming rather than with his first. It becomes an Advent prayer and watchword. It is an expression of hope rather than an affirmation of faith.

2. *The Church at worship*

But now there is another question we must consider. How is it that the apostle Paul comes to use this Aramaic expression in a letter addressed to a Greek church, without even bothering to translate it into the Greek language? There can be only one explanation. Clearly at the time when Paul wrote (about the year AD 55), the expression was well known and clearly understood throughout the churches of the Roman empire. It had become an accepted Christian password and was in common use by believers everywhere.

When was it normally used? There is good reason to believe that it was specially connected with the Church's worship, like other Aramaic words (*amen*, *hosanna*, *abba*). If so, it means that the phrase formed part of what we would now call the 'liturgy' of the Church, the worship of the Lord's supper.

This is not surprising. It is in fact what we should expect in the light of New Testament teaching. St Paul makes clear that the Lord's supper not only looks back to the cross of Jesus. It also looks forward to his coming. 'As often as you eat this bread and drink the cup, you proclaim the Lord's death until he comes'. That 'until he comes' aspect of the eucharist finds expression in this word *Maranatha*. It sums up the Church's longing for the Lord Jesus to come again in his power and glory to take his people to himself, to overthrow the forces of evil, and to establish his kingdom on earth.

3. *The advent and ourselves*

Here is a reminder of the fact that the Church in New Testament days lived in the light of the coming or *parousia* of Christ. Constantly in their minds was the thought 'The Lord is at hand', and this conviction determined their whole attitude to life and death, to their service for the Lord and to all they had to suffer for his sake.

Can we recapture something of that attitude today? Has the parousia any significance for our own lives? *What does it mean to live in the light of the Lord's coming?*

I make these three simple suggestions. For one thing, it means to have a sense of *urgency*: a realisation that time is a precious commodity and must not be wasted; that it will not last for ever and therefore must be wisely used until the Lord comes. This is the sense of St Paul's words: 'Use the present opportunity to the full, for these are evil days' (Ephesians 5.16, NEB).

For another thing, to live in the light of Christ's coming is to have a sense of *responsibility*. It determines the quality of our service and the way we live and do things now. For the Lord is coming to take account of his servants and we must live and work with loins girded and lamps burning, like men who are waiting for their master (Luke 12.35, 36). To quote St Paul again: 'We must all appear before the judgement seat of Christ, so that each one may receive good or evil, according to what he has done in the body'—that is, in this present life (2 Corinthians 5.9, 10).

Thirdly, to live in the light of the parousia is to have a sense of *expectancy*. Christianity is a religion of hope and teaches us to look forward. The coming of the Lord is part of that hope. When days are dark and the human outlook is at its worst, that hope cheers and sustains us. We can say, in the words of the Advent epistle, 'The night is far spent, the Day is at hand.' And with the Church of earliest times we can make our prayer:

Maranatha—Come, O Lord!

CHRISTMAS

Little town of Bethlehem

Luke 2.15 '*The shepherds said to one another, "Let us go over to Bethlehem and see this thing that has happened, which the Lord has made known to us."*'

At the end of 1866 Phillips Brooks, the renowned American preacher—then the youthful rector of Holy Trinity church, Philadelphia—made a pilgrimage to Palestine. On Christmas Eve he rode on horseback from Jerusalem to Bethlehem and, late at night, visited the Field of the Shepherds before joining in a service in the ancient basilica which marks the traditional site of our Lord's birth.

The experience of that night deeply impressed him, and on his return to Philadelphia he wrote a hymn for the children of his Sunday school to sing the next Christmas:

O little town of Bethlehem,
How still we see thee lie!
Above thy deep and dreamless sleep
The silent stars go by.
Yet in thy dark streets shineth
The everlasting light;
The hopes and fears of all the years
Are met in thee tonight.

The hymn focuses our attention on Bethlehem—and that is right; for at Christmas all roads lead to Bethlehem. It is at Bethlehem, historically speaking, that the story of Christmas begins. Let us journey theıe in thought for a few minutes today.

1. *The city of David*

Bethlehem was the birthplace of David, the shepherd boy who became king. For this reason Bethlehem had acquired the proud title of 'the city of David'. It was a city with associations of royalty. And it was undoubtedly one of the oldest towns in Palestine, for it is mentioned in the book of Genesis as the burial place of Rachel.

For all that, Bethlehem was not regarded as a place of outstanding importance in the history of the Jewish nation. It was indeed a 'little town' with only a small population and was almost completely overshadowed by Jerusalem, lying no more than six miles to the north. The prophet Micah recognised the comparative insignificance of the town when he uttered his well-known prophecy; but at the same time he hinted at a new glory to which Bethlehem was to attain:

> You, O Bethlehem Ephrathah,
> who are little to be among the clans of Judah,
> from you shall come forth for me
> one who is to be ruler in Israel,
> whose origin is from of old,
> from ancient days.

It was a remarkable prophecy. From the small and obscure Judean town one was to 'come forth' in the purpose of God to serve as 'ruler in Israel'. Yet while he would emerge on the scene of history in process of time, his origin was somehow wrapped in the mystery of eternity. The prophet went on (verses 3–5) to declare that this ruler would be a shepherd-king, that he would deliver his people from oppression and restore the family of Israel and bring them security and peace.

The prophecy clearly refers to the coming of the Messiah in the future—with a glance back to the past. For a shepherd-king of Israel had already 'come forth' from Bethlehem some three centuries before in the person of David. Micah now foresees the birth of great David's greater Son, and in doing so delineates some of the features of his reign.

Seven hundred years and more went by and the prophecy remained unfulfilled. Then at long last God's hour struck and once again little Bethlehem comes into view in the Bible story—this time in the narrative of the New Testament.

2. *The birthplace of Jesus*

Both Matthew and Luke, the only two evangelists to record the Nativity, expressly state that Christ was born at Bethlehem of Judaea. It didn't seem likely at first that such a thing would happen; for Mary and Joseph belonged to Nazareth in Galilee, and Nazareth is more than 70 miles to the north of Bethlehem —a considerable distance in those days.

How did it come about?

It was an imperial decree, issued by Caesar Augustus in far-off Rome, that set in motion the political machinery which brought Joseph and Mary from Nazareth to Bethlehem to take part in a census. Joseph was of the house and line of David, and therefore in accordance with Jewish custom he was required to register his name in Bethlehem, the city of David. Despite her condition, Mary made the long journey with him; and so it came about that in David's royal city 'she brought forth her firstborn son, and wrapped him in swaddling clothes, and laid him in a manger; because there was no room for them in the inn'.

The birthplace of Jesus was a stable. According to the testimony of Justin Martyr in the second century, the stable was in fact a cave. There is nothing incongruous in this tradition, for caves were commonly used as stables in those days. In a sense a stable was a fitting birthplace for him who, though he was rich, yet for our sakes became poor.

So it happened, the most momentous event in the history of the world—and 'the Word was made flesh'. Yet it happened so quietly, as Phillips Brooks reminds us in his hymn:

> How silently, how silently,
> The wondrous gift is given!
> So God imparts to human hearts
> The blessings of his heaven.

No fanfare of trumpets announced the birth of the Messiah that night. Neither great Caesar in Rome, nor Herod the Jewish puppet-king in Judaea, nor the high priest in Jerusalem, knew anything about it. But while earth slept on in darkness and silence the heavens blazed with light and rang with the song of angels—'Glory to God in the highest and peace to men on earth!'

3. *The house of bread*

It was to a band of humble shepherds guarding their flocks by night in the fields outside Bethlehem that the astonishing news was made known, and they at once embarked upon a pilgrimage. Before we follow them on their quest let us remind ourselves that the Hebrew name *Beth-lehem* means 'house of bread', or more generally 'house of food'. It refers to the fertility of the place. The surrounding hillsides provided pasture for sheep and goats, and the valleys below produced crops of barley and wheat—as in the days when Ruth gleaned there in the fields of Boaz. Bethlehem was also noted for its wine and honey. It was a place where none need be in want, where there was food in abundance and food for all.

With that thought in mind we may return to the story of the shepherds. 'Let us go over to Bethlehem and see this thing that has happened, which the Lord has made known to us.' Such was their resolve as soon as they heard the good tidings of great joy. 'And they went with haste, and found Mary and Joseph, and the babe lying in a manger.'

The shepherds were not disobedient to the heavenly vision. They came with haste: there was a sense of urgency in their quest. They came believingly and obediently, confidently taking God at his word and eagerly looking for the 'sign' that had been given them—a new-born baby lying in a manger.

Those who come to Bethlehem in the same spirit at Christmas time will never be disappointed. In the 'house of bread' they will find a satisfaction which only God can give to the hungry souls of men and which he freely offers to those who open their hearts to his love. So let Phillips Brooks have the last word as we echo his prayer:

O holy Child of Bethlehem,
  Descend to us, we pray;

Cast out our sin, and enter in:
  Be born in us today.
We hear the Christmas angels
  The great glad tidings tell;
O come to us, abide with us,
  Our Lord Emmanuel.

CHRISTMAS

The incredibility of Christmas

I Timothy 3.16 (AV) '*God manifest in the flesh.*'

When you come to think of it, it is all but incredible that the baby lying in the manger at Bethlehem was God himself . . . God in human form . . . God made man. Who would have believed it then? Who can believe it now?

Yes, when you come to *think* of it. But probably we haven't thought about it very deeply. Perhaps if we did think about it a bit more we should begin to realise how amazing the whole thing is—how apparently incredible.

Of course, in popular thought what passes for the Christmas message is nothing very extraordinary. It is little more than a pretty, sentimental tale that exudes peace and goodwill, that glorifies motherhood and sanctifies childhood, and so on. All very good as far as it goes, no doubt—and most uplifting. But scarcely incredible.

In the thought of the New Testament the birth of Jesus means something much more. It is in fact the most shattering challenge to faith.

1. *What happened*

What happened at Bethlehem was nothing less than 'the personal irruption of God into human history'. That is how Dorothy Sayers once expressed it. Or to quote our text, Jesus was 'God manifest in the flesh'. That reminds us of the Christmas Day gospel: 'The Word became flesh and dwelt among us'. The Word! But who was the Word? The evangelist tells us in quite unambiguous terms: 'The Word was God'.

Put those two sentences together and weigh them carefully:

The Word was God.
The Word became flesh.

Isn't it quite staggering? From everlasting Jesus *was* God. And when he entered this world of ours he did not cease to be God. That was impossible. But he then *became* what he had not been before—a true human being. He took upon him a body of flesh and blood like ours, derived from his mother, the Virgin Mary. So he came to us—perfect God, perfect Man.

This is the impenetrable mystery of the incarnation. God and man are united in the one person of our Lord Jesus Christ. The baby in the manger is not only Mary's child. He is God's Son. Bethlehem is the meeting-point of heaven and earth, of eternity and time, of deity and humanity.

The ancient creeds of the Church put this into theological language as they grapple with the doctrine of Christ's person: 'God, of the very substance of the Father, begotten before the worlds; and Man, of the substance of his mother, born in the world . . . who although he be God and Man, yet he is not two, but one Christ.' So the venerable Athanasian Creed.

Perhaps the language of Christian poetry may help us more than the language of theology. This is how Charles Wesley put the matter in one of his hymns of the Nativity:

Let earth and heaven combine,
Angels and men agree,
To praise in songs divine
The incarnate Deity,
Our God contracted to a span
Incomprehensibly made man.

Incomprehensible? Incredible? Yet this is what Christians

believe happened at Bethlehem. He who was 'born of a woman' was none other than 'God manifest in the flesh'.

2. *Why it happened*

But why did it happen? *Cur Deus homo?* Why did God become man?

The New Testament leaves us in no doubt about that. 'Christ Jesus came into the world to save sinners.' That was the purpose of his mission. But there is something else the New Testament makes equally clear. The saving of sinners, the reconciling of men to God, involved more than the *birth* of Jesus. It involved also his death. It meant not only his taking our flesh upon him at Bethlehem. It meant his taking our sin upon him at Calvary.

The redemption of lost mankind was beyond all human power. Only God could do it. That is why he came in the person of Jesus Christ—to do for us what we could not do for ourselves.

Martin Luther somewhere, in dealing with this matter of man's salvation, recalls Horace's rule of dramatic art, that a 'god' must not be introduced into the action of a play unless the plot has got into such a hopeless tangle that only a god could unravel it. So, says Luther, it is with man in his lost estate. Only God Almighty can rescue him and deal with his sin. That is why he became man. And that is why he died.

3. *Our own involvement*

This means we must not forget that Christmas is not the end of the story. Rather it is the beginning. And there is something else we must remember too, that we ourselves are involved in that story. It was *for us* that the Son of God came, and suffered, and triumphed. And while it is true that we cannot contribute anything to the salvation he has wrought, there *is* a response demanded from each one of us.

What sort of response? For one thing, a response of *faith*; for we are called upon to believe the incredible truth that Jesus is Emmanuel—'God with us'. And of course a response of *gratitude*, as we say from our hearts, 'Thanks be to God for his unspeakable gift!' Yes, and Christian *action* too—doing something to help those in need, and not only at Christmas but throughout the year.

But perhaps most of all at this Christmas time we need a response of sheer *wonder* as we reflect upon the amazing thing that happened. Think of it again: *God was manifest in the flesh.* Could anything be more wonderful than that? And can we do other, as we bow before the mystery of redeeming love, than pour out our hearts in a spirit of wonder, love and praise?

O come, let us adore him, Christ the Lord!

CHRISTMAS

Emmanuel

Matthew 1.22, 23 '*All this happened in order to fulfil what the Lord declared through the prophet: "The virgin shall conceive and bear a son, and he shall be called Emmanuel", a name which means "God is with us".*'

In *The Restraining Hand*, a book published in the 1930s, the story is told of two missionaries of the China Inland Mission, Bosshart and Hayman, who were taken captive by a band of Chinese brigands. Held to ransom and under the constant threat of death, they found themselves on Christmas day undergoing rigorous confinement amid bitterly cold weather. There was no fire, and the prisoners, closely guarded, were strictly forbidden to speak to one another.

As the day wore monotonously on, Bosshart suddenly recalled a word of scripture, the single word *Emmanuel*—'God with us'. It was as though God himself had spoken to his heart and he began to rejoice in spirit. He felt he must communicate the message to his companion; but how could he do so without breaking the silence? A method presented itself to him. Taking some pieces of straw which were lying around he spelled out the word on the floor: EMMANUEL.

Hayman received the message and at once the whole dismal situation underwent a transformation. 'God is with us!' The faith of the two men laid hold of the assurance and their prison became radiant with the glory of God.

Emmanuel! Let us spell out the name for ourselves this Christmas time and try to discover what message it has for us.

1. *Prophecy*

As we do so we can scarcely forget that there is *prophecy* wrapped up in this name. The evangelist introduces it into his account of the birth of the Lord Jesus by quoting an ancient oracle in the book of the prophet Isaiah: 'The virgin shall conceive and bear a son, and he shall be called Emmanuel' (Isaiah 7.14).

Considerable argument has taken place about that prophecy and how it is to be understood. I have no desire to become involved in the debate, except to remark that it's a pity that so much time has been wasted discussing whether the Hebrew word should be rendered 'young woman' or 'virgin'. Let us at least be clear that the evidence for the virgin birth of Jesus does not depend upon this obscure prophecy. In fact, the prophecy is not directly concerned with the mother at all, and only indirectly with the child. What it *is* concerned about is the *name* to be given to the child—Emmanuel. *That* was God's 'sign' to Ahaz, king of Israel. In a time of national crisis Ahaz was foolishly seeking military alliances with foreign powers instead of relying on the help of the Lord. The lesson Isaiah was trying to teach him was that the arm of flesh would fail him and that his only hope lay in divine intervention, in the saving presence of God.

It was natural enough for the early Church to see in the prophecy a reference to the birth of the promised Messiah and what it signified: God himself coming to man's rescue, God visiting and redeeming his people.

2. *Mystery*

This leads on to another thought. As we spell out the word again we recognise that there is *mystery* enshrined in the name Emmanuel: the deep, impenetrable mystery of the incarnation, the wonder of the Word made flesh. *God* with *us*—Deity united with humanity—this and nothing less than this is what the birth of Jesus means. In the person of his Son the eternal God has invaded this world of time, has emptied himself of all but love, and has been born as man.

> Hark, hark, the wise eternal Word
> Like a weak infant cries!
> In form of servant is the Lord,
> And God in cradle lies.

The good news of Christmas is that God doesn't operate, so to speak, by remote control. He was not content to love us from afar or to save us by proxy. He did not send someone else but came himself, the Maker of heaven and earth, and took our nature upon him and was born 'a little baby thing that made a woman cry'. His birthplace was a stable, his cradle a manger, his mother a lowly village maiden. Yet he was *Emmanuel*, God with us, God manifest in the flesh.

Here indeed is mystery, something too wonderful for us to understand. And we may be thankful that it is so. For if the gospel were not too big to fit into our little intellects, it would be too small to meet our vast human need. The incarnation is beyond our comprehension but not beyond our faith. Where reason cannot penetrate, love can worship and adore.

3. *Mercy*

We may go one step further. For as we spell out the word Emmanuel we can see it enshrines more than mystery. There is *mercy* shining through it too. The biggest mercy of all is here, the good news of our salvation. Emmanuel assures us that God is with us in the greatness of his redeeming love and power: that God was in Christ, reconciling the world to himself.

Matthew Henry, the Puritan commentator, said something to this effect: by the light of nature we can see God *above* us, transcendent in majesty and power; by the light of the law we see God *against* us, exercising his righteous judgement upon our guilt; but by the light of the gospel we see God *with* us and *for* us, taking our flesh that he might bear our sin, becoming one with us that we might become one with him.

The psalmist somewhere rejoices that God's mercy reaches to the heavens. We can be thankful at Christmas time that his mercy also reaches to the earth—to us and to all men, right down to the very depth of our need. As John Wesley said, the best of all is that God is with us. This is what Christmas is all about:

Veiled in flesh the Godhead see,
Hail, the incarnate Deity!
Pleased as man with man to dwell,
Jesus, our Emmanuel.

(C. Wesley)

CHRISTMAS

Love came down at Christmas

1 John 4.9. (NEB) '*God is love; and his love was disclosed to us in this, that he sent his only Son into the world to bring us life.*'

It has been said that the ordinary churchgoer learns more about the Christian faith from his hymn-book than from his Bible. At best this is only generally true; but I suspect it is specially true when it comes to that part of our faith which we celebrate at Christmas. The finest of our hymns and carols have much to teach us here. Of course, they are meant to be poetry, not theology. Yet they help us to understand, in language we can grasp, the real meaning of the birth of the Lord Jesus and why he came into the world.

Let me give you an example. In one of her tenderest poems, Christina Rossetti interprets the mystery of the incarnation in this way:

> Love came down at Christmas,
> Love all lovely, Love divine;
> Love was born at Christmas,
> Star and angels gave the sign.

1. *Love's disclosure*

It's an exhilarating thought that the story of Christmas is the story of Love incarnate. The good news which rings out in the New Testament is not simply that 'God is love'—as though it were love in the abstract. The good news is that in the person of Jesus Christ the love of God has appeared on earth in visible form, clothed in the garment of our humanity. The 'Word which God addresses to men in the gospel is Love; and 'the Word was made flesh and dwelt among us, full of grace and truth.'

Yes, Love came down at Christmas. Christina Rossetti's song is but an echo of St John's words in my text: 'God is love; and his love was disclosed to us in this, that he sent his only Son into the world to bring us life.'

Here is Love's disclosure. Christmas tells us what God is like. It answers the questions which have always haunted the minds of men when they have thought deeply about ultimate reality. Assuming there is a God, and that it is he who made us and the world in which we live, what kind of a God is he? What is his attitude to man? How does he feel about this world of sinning, suffering humanity? Does he really care for us? Is he able and willing to help us?

The answer to these questions is to be found in the birth of Mary's child that first Christmas night. Back of all the mystery of the incarnation, back of all the sentiment that has gathered round the Christmas story, back of all the joy that fills our hearts at this season, stands the supreme, majestic fact that 'God loved the world so much that he gave his only Son . . . '.

Love came down at Christmas when a baby was born to a poor Jewish woman in a cattle-shed, wrapped round with swaddling bands and laid in a manger. It was the God of Love himself entering our world, penetrating our common life, coming into our midst in such a way that his love might be a thing of flesh and blood, a concrete, visible reality.

2. *Love's mission*

This at once raises a question. Why, in the poet's words, was Love born at Christmas, 'Love all lovely, Love divine'? The poem itself does not answer the question. But our text does. God sent his Son into the world, says St John, *to bring us life.*

It's an arresting answer. Let's take note of it in case we miss the whole meaning of Christmas. For Christ didn't come into the world simply to reform society or to give man a little moral boost. He came to bring us life. He came to save sinners. Only a complete misreading of the New Testament can explain away the redemptive mission of the Son of God. And only a hopelessly mistaken view of man—modern man, man come of age—can deny that man is in desperate need of redemption.

Love came down to lift us up. That's the deepest meaning of the Christmas story. It was all 'for us men and for our salvation'. As Charles Wesley puts it in his great Christmas hymn, Christ was

> Born to raise the sons of earth,
> Born to give them second birth.

No less a purpose than this is sufficient to account for the stupendous miracle of Incarnate Love. Man is fallen and needs to be raised again to his high estate. Man is dead in sin and needs to be reborn to life eternal. It was for this that Love Divine took our flesh and dwelt among us and went to the cross. Love came to bring us life. Such was Love's mission.

3. *Love's demand*

There is one other question. What of Love's demand? And

here Christina Rossetti does provide an answer. There can in fact be only one answer:

Worship we the Godhead,
  Love Incarnate, Love Divine;
Worship we our Jesus:
  But wherewith for sacred sign?

Love shall be our token,
  Love be yours and love be mine,
Love to God and all men,
  Love for plea and gift and sign.

If the love of God revealed in the Christmas event is true and not just a pious legend or a bit of wishful thinking, then we can do nothing else than worship: worship the God who is Love Incarnate and whose Love came down at Christmas.

Rossetti saw so clearly that Love demands love. And this, of course, is what St John says: 'If God thus loved us, dear friends, we in turn are bound to love one another.' And again: 'We love because he loved us first.' And yet again: 'If a man says, "I love God", while hating his brother, he is a liar. If he does not love the brother whom he has seen, it cannot be that he loves God whom he has not seen.'

Rossetti was right. Love's demand is for love—'Love to God and all men, Love for plea and gift and sign.'

Love for *plea*? Yes; for love enables us to approach God with confidence and banishes fear. And love for *gift*? Indeed; for just as love is God's gift to us, so it must be ours to others. And love for *sign*? Of course! What other sign do we need? For love is the authentic mark of our profession, the sign by which the world recognises whose we are and whom we serve.

Here is the supreme challenge of the Christmas mystery.

EPIPHANY

The quest of the magi

Matthew 2.2 (NEB) ' "*Where is the child who is born to be king of the Jews? We observed the rising of his star, and we have come to pay him homage.*" '

The magi or 'wise men' in the Epiphany story were doubtless religious astrologers who studied the stars, in the belief that the movements of the heavenly bodies reflected the destinies of men. The eastern land from which they came was probably Arabia or Persia. More than that we cannot say with any degree of certainty. For the rest, we are thrown back on the record of St Matthew's gospel, which tells of their quest for a new-born king and of their eventual arrival in Bethlehem.

How did it all come about? By what light were they guided on their way?

1. *The light of nature*

In the beginning they were directed on their long journey by the light of a star. 'Where is the child who is born to be king of the Jews?' they asked when they entered Jerusalem. 'We observed the rising of his star, and we have come to pay him homage.'

There has been a good deal of speculation about the appearing of the so-called star of Bethlehem. Astronomers have suggested that it may have been due to the rare conjunction of Jupiter, Saturn and Venus in the year 7 BC. At any rate, it created a profound impression on the magi and for reasons not stated they came to the conclusion that it heralded the birth of a new king of Israel. So they set out on their pilgrimage to the land of the Jews.

Initially, then, the star was the only light they had. Surely we are not being fanciful when we say that, as far as these Gentiles were concerned, the star represents the light of nature. It's always well to remember that there is such a thing as natural religion. What the psalmist said is true: 'The heavens declare the glory of God'. St Paul speaks about this in his letter to the Romans when he condemns the pagan world of his day for its ignorance of God; for, as he says, God's invisible nature can be clearly perceived in the things that have been made. (See Romans 1.19–23.) In a word, the Creator is revealed in the works of creation.

The light of nature, the light of conscience, the light of human reason—these may not take us very far in our search for truth, but they can at least provide a starting point. The star which the magi saw gave them enough light to enable them to begin their quest.

2. *The light of scripture*

'Where is the child who is born to be king of the Jews?' Obviously these men expected they would find the infant king in Jerusalem itself, the Jewish capital. Where else would he be born? Equally obviously they expected the whole city to be rejoicing in the king's birth. But their question met with blank astonishment. No one knew of any new-born king. The Jewish leaders, it seemed, showed very little interest. The people were troubled and perplexed. It was Herod the Great, puppet king of Israel under the Roman jurisdiction, who expressed most concern—and that purely out of self-interest.

Herod was an intensely jealous man. When the report reached him he was deeply perturbed at the thought of a rival to his throne. He knew well enough that a Messiah-King was expected by the Jews, but he was too ignorant of his Bible to know where he was to be born. So he summoned the religious experts and put his question to them. They answered his inquiry by referring him to an ancient prophecy of Micah, who had declared that the Messiah would emerge from Bethlehem (Micah 5.2).

Here was fuller light than the magi possessed. The eastern astrologers had consulted the *stars*. The Jewish teachers were able to consult the *scriptures*. And the scriptures provided the answer to the question they had been asked.

The Bible is like that. It is a book that answers our questions:

not all of them, indeed, nor always in the detailed way we would like. But it *has* an answer and it points us in the right direction when we turn to it with an honest faith To us, still, God's Word is a lamp to our feet and a light to our path.

The magi were now able to pursue their quest a stage further. Guided by the light of revelation and acting under Herod's urgent directions, they left Jerusalem and made their way to Bethlehem, six miles to the south.

3. *The light of Christ*

'They set out at the king's bidding; and the star which they had seen at its rising went ahead of them until it stopped above the place where the child lay. At the sight of the star they were overjoyed.' The star's guidance was not actually needed for this last stage of the journey; but its reappearance assured them that their search was about to meet with success. And it led them to the very house in Bethlehem where the new-born King was to be found.

'Entering the house, they saw the child with Mary his mother, and bowed to the ground in homage to him. Then they opened their treasures and offered him gifts: gold, frankincense, and myrrh.' For the magi this was the end of a long quest. It had begun many months earlier in their far-off eastern country. It finished in the presence of the Christ-child, the Word made flesh. As we see them bowing before him, offering their homage and presenting their gifts, we recognise that here is a piece of prophetic symbolism. The magi represent the first fruits of the nations seeking and finding the Christ, who came

> to be a light to lighten the Gentiles,
> and to be the glory of God's people Israel.

That light, the light of Christ, still shines for us in our dark world; and it beckons onwards all who in our day tread the pilgrim path, searching for the secret of life, for ultimate reality. The quest for truth may be a long one, but it is not an endless one. There is an end to the journey and the end is Jesus.

That is why he declared, 'I am the way; I am the truth and I am the life; no one comes to the Father except by me.'

EPIPHANY

The baptism of Jesus

> Mark 1.10, 11 '*When he came up out of the water, immediately he saw the heavens opened and the Spirit descending upon him like a dove; and a voice came from heaven, "Thou art my beloved Son; with thee I am well pleased."*'

We in our churches today instinctively connect the feast of the Epiphany with the story of the wise men and what the Prayer Book calls 'the manifestation of Christ to the Gentiles'. But in the Eastern Church, where the feast originates—and its origin goes right back to the third century—the Epiphany was held in honour of our Lord's birth and baptism. It marked both his manifestation as the Word made flesh, God in human form, and his manifestation to the people of Israel some thirty years later when he embarked upon his public ministry and was baptised in the river Jordan.

There is no other festival in the Church's year which commemorates the baptism of Jesus, and we are surely right to let the Epiphany do this for us. What has the story to say to us?

The gospel accounts mention three 'signs' which accompanied the baptism and which may help to interpret its meaning. We will look at them in turn.

1. *The opened heaven*

When news of the preaching of John the Baptist and the religious revival which accompanied it reached Nazareth in Galilee, Jesus knew that the long-awaited hour had struck. He must leave his village home and the carpenter's bench and go south. So he came to the Jordan where John was preaching his message of judgement, calling upon the people to repent and to wash away their sins in baptism and to make themselves ready for the coming of God's kingdom.

At the end of it all Jesus presented himself for baptism. Mark's pictorial account of what happened is vivid and arresting. At the moment when Jesus came up out of the water 'he saw the heavens torn open', as the NEB puts it.

What did it mean, that opened heaven? It bore witness, I believe, to the perfect humanity of Jesus. To man in his sinful state heaven is closed, and must be closed, for heaven is the abode of the holy. But to *this* man, the man Christ Jesus, as he presents himself in his pure, unsullied humanity and dedicates himself to his saving mission as God's Messiah, heaven is opened. There is nothing in this man of which heaven can disapprove. 'Heaven, which must for ever exclude what is imperfect, could then have enfolded Jesus without violation of any principle of Eternal Holiness' (G. Campbell Morgan).

This at once raises an important question. If Jesus was such, why was he baptised? For John's baptism was a baptism of *repentance*. It was for sinners only. The sinless Christ had nothing of which to repent. What part had he in John's baptism? The answer is this. At the very outset of his ministry, Jesus made himself one with those he came to save. As he went down into the Jordan he took his stand by the side of sinners and was numbered with the transgressors. It was an act of self-identification which found its culmination at Calvary when he took upon himself the sin of the world and carried it away for ever.

2. *The descent of the dove*

At his baptism Jesus saw 'the Spirit, like a dove, descending upon him'. Here is another piece of symbolism—heaven's response to the Lord's dedication to service.

We may think of it in terms of divine investiture. Jesus was endowed with the Holy Spirit to equip him for the mission he was called to fulfil as the promised Messiah. We must remember that the word Messiah or *Christos* means 'anointed'. In Old Testament times, priests and kings were anointed with oil and solemnly consecrated or set apart for the office they were to fulfil.

In his baptism the Lord Jesus as God's Messiah is anointed with the Spirit for his priestly and kingly role. So he enters upon his ministry, as Luke tells us, 'in the power of the Spirit'. But it's worth noting that the Spirit that rests upon him is the gentle Spirit of purity and meekness. This is signified by the dove. Jesus exercises his ministry among men in the strength of gentleness. He conquers their hearts by the omnipotence of love.

All this has plenty of meaning for us, if we have eyes to see. For Jesus at his baptism represents the pattern man. What was true for him then in fullest measure may be equally true for us in lesser degree. We may be sure that God never withholds his Spirit from those who give themselves to him. When he calls us to do any work for him he gives us strength for the task; and that strength is found in his own gracious Spirit of purity and love.

3. *The voice of the Father*

The third sign at the baptism was vocal. After the vision came the voice—the voice which spoke from heaven: 'Thou art my beloved Son; with thee I am well pleased.' It was the voice of the Father, speaking directly to Jesus, designating him as his Son, the Beloved, and expressing approval of him as he set his face to accomplish his messianic mission.

It is clear that what happened at the baptism, as described in the gospels, must have come from Jesus himself. The experience that befell him was an intensely personal one. The vision he saw gave him a new consciousness of spiritual power and the voice he heard afforded him a deep inner confirmation of his Sonship and Messiahship.

One thing more remains to be said. The whole scene set before us in the baptism story is an *epiphaneia*, a manifestation of Christ, marking him out as the perfect Man, the promised

Messiah, the divine Son. But not only that. It is also a manifestation of God in his triune glory. The three persons of the Trinity are present and active in the baptism. The dedication of the incarnate Son is accompanied by the anointing of the Holy Spirit and the attestation of the heavenly Father.

What can we say to this? Nothing! We can only bow our hearts in wonder as we worship the Lord in the beauty of holiness.

PASSIONTIDE

PASSION SUNDAY

Looking at the cross

Galatians 6.14 '*God forbid that I should glory, save in the cross of our Lord Jesus Christ, by whom the world is crucified unto me, and I unto the world.*'

Beyond question one of the greatest passion hymns is Isaac Watts's 'When I survey the wondrous cross'. Matthew Arnold considered it to be the finest hymn in the English language. Watts published it in 1707 under the title: 'Crucifixion to the world by the cross of Christ. Galatians 6.14.' It was intended as a hymn for the Lord's supper.

What is Watts doing in this hymn? He is looking at the cross of Jesus. And that is what we are called upon to do on this Passion Sunday: to take a fresh look at the cross and to allow its message to penetrate our hearts and minds.

I believe Watts's hymn may help us to do this. It's a hymn full of instruction. It shows us what to see in the cross—what the passion of our Lord should mean to us.

1. *The cross—the ground of all our boasting*

In the first place, it shows us that the cross is the ground of all our boasting as Christians. In its original version it began:

When I survey the wondrous cross
 Where the young Prince of glory died.

In the second edition a couple of years later, Watts altered the second line to its present form: 'On which the Prince of glory died.' This was probably done in response to the criticism of certain friends.

Some will regret that the change was made. There is after all something appealing in the reference to the *young* Prince of glory. It reminds us that Christ died when still a young man and that Christianity itself began as something in the nature of a youth movement. Somehow we don't often think of that. We are inclined to regard the Church as a musty institution, an antiquarian society, an old people's club. It has lost the bloom and vigour of its youth.

What happens when a man looks at the young Prince of glory hanging on the cross, bearing away the sin of the world? The answer is that the sight robs him of every bit of self-satisfaction and self-esteem:

My richest gain I count but loss,
 And pour contempt on all my pride.

'*My richest gain*'—note the phrase. There is obviously a reference here to St Paul's words, 'What things were gain to me, those I counted loss for Christ' (Philippians 3.7). When the apostle wrote that, he was looking back to his old life as a self-righteous Pharisee, recalling the treasury of personal merit he had hoarded up in an attempt to make himself acceptable to God. In the light of the cross he saw it all as sheer loss, as so much worthless rubbish. He poured contempt on all his pride. He gloried only in what the Lord had done for him.

Forbid it, Lord, that I should boast,
 Save in the death of Christ my God!
All the vain things that charm me most,
 I sacrifice them to his blood.

This second verse is a direct echo of Paul's words which inspired the hymn, 'God forbid that I should glory, save in the cross of our Lord Jesus Christ'. He saw in the cross, as God's saving act, the thing of supreme worth. Compared with it, all other things were secondary—'vain things', however much they might charm the soul.

When we look with understanding at Calvary we get our sense of values right. We begin to see what matters—and what doesn't. Above all, we recognise that the ground of all our hope is Christ and him crucified. We boast of him, not of ourselves.

2. *The cross—the revelation of the heart of God*

When we look at the cross again we see an unveiling of the heart of God:

> See from his head, his hands, his feet,
> Sorrow and love flow mingled down;
> Did e'er such love and sorrow meet,
> Or thorns compose so rich a crown?

In St John's gospel we are told that a soldier, to prove that Jesus was dead, pierced his side with a spear, 'and forthwith there came out blood and water'. Watts, with a touch of poetic imagination, gazes at the terrible scene and sees not blood and water but 'sorrow and love flow mingled down'. What is the significance of that?

Surely the *sorrow* of the Saviour on the cross was sorrow for *sin*: the sin of the world for which he suffered and died. He was a 'man of sorrows and acquainted with grief' because he was 'wounded for our transgressions' and the Lord 'laid on him the iniquity of us all'. So equally surely the *love* of the Saviour on the cross was love for the *sinner*. Let us never forget that while it was our sin that took him to the cross, it was his love for us that held him there—not the nails of the Roman soldiers.

'Did e'er such love and sorrow meet?' Well may we ask that question. And also the next: 'Or thorns compose so rich a crown?' To Christian faith, as it bows in adoration at the cross, the worthless wreath of thorns on the Saviour's brow is transformed into a glittering diadem, a monarch's crown. The Man of Sorrows is the King of Love.

3. *The cross—the measure of our indebtedness to Christ*

No hymn rises to such sublime heights of devotion as does this in its final verse where it confronts us with the claims of redeeming love:

> Were the whole realm of nature mine,
> That were a present far too small;
> Love so amazing, so divine,
> Demands my soul, my life, my all.

In the cross we see the measure of our indebtedness to Christ. That is why Calvary demands a verdict—and a response. We cannot look at the cross and remain neutral or impassive. We are eternally in debt to Christ. He gave everything for us. What are we to give to him? 'The whole realm of nature' to which the hymn refers is not in fact ours to give. But even if it were, it would not be an adequate return for so immeasurable a sacrifice.

There is only one thing we can give, and it must be a personal offering: 'my soul, my life, my all.' My *soul* is what I am, the essence of my individual being. My *life* is what I do, my day-to-day labours and activities. My *all* is what I have, my gifts and talents, my wealth and possessions. The claim of redeeming love is total.

St Francis realised this when, as a young man of twenty-four, in a state of great spiritual uncertainty, he caught a vision of the Crucified. At the time he was praying in the little ruined church of St Damian, just outside the walls of Assisi. As he gazed at a wooden crucifix behind the altar he became transfixed. It was as though Christ appeared to him and spoke to him from the cross and demanded his life. Francis yielded. From that moment he became the servant of his crucified Lord and vowed he would spend all his days in the service of Christ's poor brethren. He had given his answer:

Love so amazing, so divine,
Demands my soul, my life, my all.

PASSIONTIDE

PALM SUNDAY

The King enters his city

Matthew 21.8, 9 '*Most of the crowd spread their garments on the road, and others cut branches from the trees and spread them on the road. And the crowds that went before him and that followed him shouted, "Hosanna to the Son of David! Blessed be he who comes in the name of the Lord! Hosanna in the highest!"*'

It's odd to reflect today that the demonstrations and marches which are so familiar a feature of our modern life are nothing new. They go back at least to the first Palm Sunday. What happened then as Jesus entered Jerusalem, 'the city of the great King', was a noisy and lively affair, with a lot of shouting and singing and waving of branches (the equivalent of our modern banners) and spreading garments on the road.

Small wonder the Jewish authorities were thoroughly annoyed, especially as the affair claimed to be a religious demonstration. This wasn't the way the established church did things. It was all most improper and undignified. Besides which, there were obviously sinister political elements underlying the whole business—and the political situation was already difficult and dangerous enough.

It is against this sort of background that we must view the story and watch the lowly yet majestic figure of Jesus riding into Jerusalem on a donkey. How do we see him?

1. *His courage*

To begin with, we can scarcely fail to be impressed by his courage. When Jesus entered Jerusalem that day he was moving forward of deliberate purpose to his last and most bitter conflict. He knew full well what was ahead, yet he never flinched. His enemies in the city were plotting to destroy him. He was a wanted man. There was a price on his head. Prudence would have counselled him to keep away, or at any rate to have acted secretly.

But the time for secrecy was now past and Jesus knew no fear. Earlier, Luke tells us, he had 'set his face to go to Jerusalem'. With resolution and determination he had made the journey south in the company of his disciples.

Now the moment of crisis has come. He has reached the mount of Olives. Jerusalem lies before him. He sends two of the disciples to borrow an ass, and, to the acclamation of the crowd, he boldly rides into the city to meet the murderous hatred of the Pharisees and Sadducees and the whole Jewish hierarchy. There is magnificent courage here.

2. *His poverty*

When Jesus wished to enter his city in royal estate he did so on a borrowed beast of burden. He had nothing of his own he could use for the purpose. The King of Glory was a pauper king on earth. 'You know the grace of our Lord Jesus Christ', wrote St Paul, 'that though he was rich, yet for your sake he became poor.' The gospels provide an apt commentary on that statement. When he was born he was laid in a borrowed manger. When he died he was buried in a borrowed tomb. Now for his royal progress into the holy city he rides on a borrowed donkey.

Some regard the story of the borrowing of the animal as an instance of our Lord's foreknowledge. It seems more natural to believe that he had a prearranged understanding with a friend at Bethphage and that he was now carrying out a plan which they had mutually agreed upon some time before. Perhaps the password was, 'The Lord has need of it'. In Mark's account there is an interesting variation: 'If any one says to you, "Why are you doing this?" say, "The Lord has need of it and will send it back here immediately".' Jesus only wished to *borrow* the beast. He was too poor to buy it. He therefore promised that it would be returned safely later on.

3. *His humility*

By coming to Jerusalem in the way he did Jesus was clearly asserting his kingship: presenting himself to his people as their Messiah. At the same time he was making clear the character of his messiahship. The key to his action is found in the prophecy of Zechariah 9.9:

> Rejoice greatly, O daughter of Zion!
> Shout aloud, O daughter of Jerusalem!
> Lo, your king comes to you;
> triumphant and victorious is he,
> humble and riding on an ass,
> on a colt, the foal of an ass.

It is significant that Jesus did not come to Jerusalem riding on a *horse*—the symbol of war. He rode on an *ass*, the symbol of peace. He was accompanied by no armed forces brandishing swords. His companions were a bunch of simple peasants waving branches of palm. Probably it was a somewhat unimposing spectacle. Imperial Rome would not have been much impressed by the sight.

Yet clearly Jesus took this line of set purpose. By acting out the prophecy of Zechariah he was making plain the kind of king he was—and the kind of kingdom he had come to establish. He comes as the king meek and lowly. He comes not to make war on the Romans but to win a great spiritual conquest, to redeem men from the bondage of sin and Satan, to exercise his rule of love in the hearts of his people.

The Jewish authorities would have nothing of this. It didn't match up with their ideas of messiahship. So they rejected him. Before the end of the week he was crucified, dead, and buried.

4. *His majesty*

What then are we to make of the Palm Sunday episode? Was the whole thing something of a fiasco and did it all end in failure? Certainly not! This was the Lord's hour of triumph, the prelude to the ultimate triumph of Easter day.

'Lo, your king comes to you!' the prophet had foretold, and it was as king that Jesus came. For a brief moment his true majesty was revealed and acclaimed. How far the shouting and palm-waving crowd grasped the meaning of it all we do not know, but clearly they sensed that this was a royal occasion and for very joy they cried out, 'Hosanna to the Son of David! Blessed is the King who comes in the name of the Lord!' Of course the Pharisees didn't like it and protested vigorously: 'Teacher, reprimand your disciples!' Jesus answered, 'I tell you, if these were silent, the very stones would cry out.'

Nothing could stop it. As Bishop Moorman comments, 'On this day and at this hour God in Christ must be worshipped.' And concerning the reference to the stones crying out he has this to say:

> The Roman authorities tried to prevent the early Christians from performing acts of worship which they thought were disloyal; but, while they were busy destroying those whom they had caught, others were meeting underground or in secret in little chapels where the worship of God went on and 'the stones cried out', echoing their praises. So it has always been, and always will be. . . . God must be worshipped.

How true that is! And this is why on this Palm Sunday we bring our worship to our King and adore his majesty and offer him 'all glory, laud and honour'.

> The people of the Hebrews
> With palms before him went;
> Our praise and prayer and anthems
> Before him we present.

PASSIONTIDE

MAUNDY THURSDAY

The feast of the new covenant

Matthew 26.28 ' "*This is my blood of the covenant, which is poured out for many for the forgiveness of sins.*" '

It is the night before the Lord's passion—'the same night in which he was betrayed'. With his disciples Jesus has gathered in an upper room in Jerusalem to observe the passover; and on this Maundy Thursday evening we gather in spirit with them. Indeed, whenever we celebrate the holy communion we are in a sense repeating or reproducing what was done then. The scene in the upper room provides the pattern of the eucharist and the clue to its meaning.

It is therefore important that we should observe carefully what took place on that occasion. What are the essential elements in the story?

1. *The presence of Jesus*

The most significant thing without doubt is that the Lord Jesus was there, presiding at the table. I feel sure that this is what filled the minds of the disciples in that solemn hour—the presence of their Master. Their eyes were fixed on him. They were more conscious of him than of one another. For them, this was truly the *Lord's* supper. He was the host, they were his guests.

When as Christians we now share together in the sacrament, we surely know something at least of the same experience. However much scholars may quarrel over the theology of the 'real presence', there is little dispute among ordinary believers as to its reality. In fact, we most commonly call the sacrament the *holy communion*—for the very reason that it is a means of communion or fellowship with Christ. 'The cup of blessing which we bless, is it not a participation in the blood of Christ?

The bread which we break, is it not a participation in the body of Christ?'

The story is told of an old Scotswoman who when the family reached home after a communion service would ask the younger members, 'Did you meet anyone in the service?' They would most likely respond by mentioning various friends and neighbours they had met; whereupon she would press her question with gentle insistence: 'Yes, I know about those, but did you meet *anyone in particular* in the service?' They knew then that she was thinking of the Lord himself.

Is that how we think of the Lord's supper, as a trysting-place with Christ? Do we find his presence near us? Charles Wesley wrote in one of his sacramental hymns:

Our hearts we open wide
  To make the Saviour room;
And lo! the Lamb, the Crucified,
  The sinner's Friend, is come.

Thy presence makes the feast;
  Now let our spirits feel
The glory not to be expressed,
  The joy unspeakable.

2. *The actions of Jesus*

The next significant thing to note is what Jesus did. To begin with, he 'took bread'—the unleavened bread of the passover; for this was in some form a passover meal, commemorating Israel's deliverance from the bondage of Egypt through the death of the lamb slain for each household. Jesus was about to accomplish a yet greater redemption for mankind by *his* death as the Lamb of God; so when he took the bread he *broke* it and said, 'This is my body which is given for you'. The early Christians saw something full of meaning in that action, for they called the Lord's supper 'the breaking of bread'. They remembered that Jesus had broken the bread in the upper room, and they realised that this foreshadowed the breaking of his body on the cross for the world's salvation.

The Lord's other action at the feast also pointed to his passion. He took a cup of wine and when he had offered thanks to God he gave it to the disciples to drink, telling them that it represented 'the blood of the covenant' which was to be shed for the forgiveness of sins.

3. *The words of Jesus*

It is impossible to separate these actions of Jesus from his words, some of which we have already quoted. We must now look a little more closely as what he said as he gave the disciples the bread and wine.

The bread, he said, was his *body*. The wine, he said, was his *blood*. He meant of course that the bread and wine were the sacred emblems of his passion. But he said something else as well. He said that the bread which was his body the disciples were to take and *eat*, and the wine which was his blood they were to *drink*, all of them.

By this he clearly meant that they were to *participate* in his sacrifice: to appropriate the benefits of his passion and to make those benefits their own. This is why in the sacrament the bread and wine are not only offered to us but *received* by us, that we may feed upon Christ in our hearts by faith with thanksgiving.

One other thing. Jesus spoke of the wine as 'the blood of the covenant'—that is, of the new covenant he was about to inaugurate; and he added, 'I shall not again drink of the fruit of the vine until that day when I drink it new in the kingdom of God'. So he associated the feast both with the *covenant* and with the *kingdom*. What did he mean? The covenant speaks of the *new relationship* with God into which we enter through our Lord's perfect and once-for-all sacrifice; and the kingdom speaks of the *new community* to which we belong as we share in the covenant—that kingdom which is 'righteousness and peace and joy in the Holy Spirit'.

CONCLUSION

Enough has been said to show the close connection between

what happened on that first Maundy Thursday evening in the upper room and what happens now when we obey the Lord's command, 'Do this in remembrance of me'.

> We meet, as in that upper room they met:
> Thou at the table, blessing, yet dost stand—

so runs a couplet in Canon Briggs's hymn; and as we meet we too find ourselves in the presence of the Lord Jesus, enjoying communion with him; we remember his passion and give thanks for his redeeming love; we enter into the mystery of his sacrifice and share by faith in what he has done for us; we bind ourselves to God in the covenant of his grace and deepen our fellowship with one another as members of the new community.

PASSIONTIDE

GOOD FRIDAY

The centrality of the cross

John 19.18 '*They crucified him, and with him two others, on either side one, and Jesus in the midst.*'

Three crosses were set up on Golgatha that first Good Friday. The gospels all make this clear. They tell us that two brigands guilty of murder were put to death with Jesus. But St John's gospel alone adds this revealing detail, that the two criminals were crucified on either side of Jesus, with *Jesus in the midst.*

What the writer is making clear is that Jesus occupied the central cross, and for him this was something that possessed deep significance. His words are more than a bare statement of fact. They are charged with a symbolical and mystical meaning. They are intended to indicate the centrality of the cross in the Christian scheme. For the Church, the crucified Son of God is always 'in the midst'—the living centre of its faith, the glowing heart of its worship, the abiding pattern of its life and mission.

1. *Central to the Church's faith*

Certainly the cross is central to the Church's *faith*. It lies at the very heart of the gospel. The cross is not simply *a* truth of the gospel, one among many. It is the essential and primary truth. Listen to St Paul as he puts the Christians at Corinth in mind of the faith he had delivered to them and which they had received:

> I delivered to you as of first importance what I also received, that Christ died for our sins in accordance with the scriptures, that he was buried, that he was raised on the third day in accordance with the scriptures (1 Corinthians 15.3, 4).

Of *first importance* this—'that Christ died for our sins'. For the apostle, the cross constituted a priority. It was of the very essence of the gospel. And this is in harmony with the New Testament teaching as a whole. Leave the cross out of the gospel and you have no gospel left; for it is the cross that makes the gospel God's 'good news' to men—the ultimate and only answer to the bad news of human guilt and despair.

Why is this? Because the cross declares that 'God was in Christ reconciling the world to himself'. It insists that 'Christ died for sins once for all, the Righteous One for the unrighteous, that he might bring us to God'. It points us to Jesus as the Lamb of God who has taken away the sin of the world, as our great High Priest who has offered 'one sacrifice for sin for ever', as the one who knew no sin yet was himself 'made sin' for us.

Who can grasp the mystery of it all? The atonement is beyond our understanding. Yet it lies at the very centre of our faith. What then are we to do about it? Not to try to explain it or rationalise it but simply to accept it. Let us remind ourselves on this Good Friday that the death of Christ is not so much a piece of theology to be critically examined, but a saving truth to be humbly and gratefully received by faith.

2. *Central to the Church's worship*

As the cross is central to the Church's faith, so it is also to the Church's *worship*. The adoration of the Lamb is characteristic to the whole Church of God, in heaven and on earth.

> 'Worthy the Lamb that died,' they cry,
> 'To be exalted thus!'
> 'Worthy the Lamb,' our lips reply,
> 'For he was slain for us!'

On this solemn day we can scarcely forget that it was on the night before his passion, 'the same night in which he was betrayed', that the Lord Jesus took the bread and wine and invested them with a new spiritual value as the sacrament of his body and blood. Ever since then, for well over 1,900 years, that sacrament has been the focal point of Christian devotion, the divinely appointed memorial of the Saviour's death and passion, the pledge of his abiding presence with his people. He is always 'in the midst' of the worshipping community.

Where the Lord's supper is central in the Church's worship, the cross is also central. For the sacrament was given to us (to quote some words from the Prayer Book seldom heard nowadays) 'to the end that we should always remember the exceeding great love of our Master and only Saviour Jesus Christ, thus dying for us, and the unnumerable benefits which by his precious blood-shedding he hath obtained for us'.

3. *Central to the Church's life and mission*

Just as Jesus is 'in the midst' of our faith and worship, so is he also of our *life and mission*. What do I mean by that? I mean this: that the Church goes out into the world to live under the shadow of the cross, bearing the marks of the Lord Jesus and testifying by word and deed to the faith of Christ crucified.

The apostle Paul put it like this: 'I have been crucified with Christ; it is no longer I who live but Christ who lives in me; and the life I now live in the flesh I live by faith in the Son of God, who loved me and gave himself for me'.

Let's be clear that the cross is more than a sign to be made, a symbol to be displayed, an ornament to be worn. It is the mark of our identification with Christ and it therefore determines the quality of our discipleship. It demands a life of love and sacrifice and self-denial. But more than that. It calls us to engage in mission and provides us with both the missionary motive and the missionary message.

The evangel of the cross is itself the final argument for evangelism. The very fact that Christ died for the sins of the whole world necessarily makes the Church into a missionary body. What Christ has done for all must be made known to all. Here then is our motive. And here also is our message. 'We preach Christ crucified, a stumbling-block to Jews (the self-righteous people) and folly to Greeks (the intellectually proud), but to those who are called, both Jews and Greeks, Christ the power of God and the wisdom of God.'

EASTER

The third day

1 Corinthians 15.4 '*He was raised on the third day in accordance with the scriptures.*'

A small boy was gazing into the window of a picture shop. A gentleman passing by stopped beside him and saw that the boy was looking intently at a picture of the crucifixion.

'Do you know who that is?' he asked.

'Yes, sir,' said the boy. 'That's Jesus. They put him to death.'

The gentleman nodded and went on his way. But he hadn't gone far when he heard footsteps behind him and the boy came running after him.

'Excuse me, sir,' he said. 'I forgot to tell you—*he didn't stay dead!*'

The boy was right. The story of the New Testament doesn't end with Good Friday. Had it done so, it would have ended altogether. Had it done so, there would in fact be no New Testament at all. Nobody would have thought of writing the story of Jesus if he had remained dead.

'The third day he was raised from the dead.' That's the good news as St Paul recalls it here in his letter to the Church at Corinth.

1. *The Easter fact*

In the passage from which our text is taken the apostle is dealing with the great historical facts on which the gospel rests. He mentions three such facts concerning Christ:

> first, that he *died* for our sins;
> second, that he was *buried*;
> third, that he was *raised* on the third day.

Paul had no doubt that Christ died, for only so could he deal with our sins. Likewise he is insistent that Christ was buried, for this was proof that he had really died. But the crowning truth to which he points is this, 'that he was raised on the third day in accordance with the scriptures'.

The third day! Note the dogmatic certainty of this apostolic confession of faith. There is nothing vague or indefinite about our Lord's resurrection. The New Testament is quite positive about its historical reality. It treats it as an event which happened at a particular point in time.

On the *first* day Jesus died on the cross and was buried. On the *second* day his body rested in Joseph's rock-hewn tomb. And on the *third* day he rose from the dead and showed himself alive to his disciples.

What form did his resurrection take? Obviously the same form as his death and burial. The three facts which Paul mentions here must all be interpreted in the same way. When Paul says 'he was raised on the third day' he means that Christ's resurrection was the same sort of fact as his death and burial. It really happened—on the third day. The body which had died and been laid to rest was no longer in the tomb. The tomb was empty.

All this makes nonsense of the argument—if it can be called an argument—that the early Church was not interested in what happened to the body of Jesus, and that the empty tomb is to be regarded as a spiritual symbol, not as a literal fact. The witness of the New Testament is quite decisive here. The fourth gospel is especially emphatic—and its evidence is all the more impressive in that this gospel is usually regarded as being more concerned with spiritual truth than with historical happenings. It tells of how two of the apostles actually entered the tomb and carried out an on-the-spot investigation. They found only the grave clothes. The body of Jesus was not there. On the third day he was raised from the dead!

2. *The Easter faith*

What a day that was—the third day! For the enemies of Jesus it was a day of the utmost confusion and consternation. Just when they thought they had finally got him safely out of the way there were these alarming reports that he was alive and at large—and that the tomb, so carefully sealed and guarded, was empty.

The victory of Jesus spelt defeat for his enemies.

For the disciples it meant something very different. The third day on which he was raised from the dead was the day when God's honour was vindicated: the day when Christ's great triumph over sin and death and the powers of darkness was demonstrated to the world. It was the day when man's salvation was secured once and for all: the day when he who was delivered up for our offences was raised again for our justification.

It was the day when the Church's hope was born—the hope which enables the believer to face life and all the unknown future with a song of trust, to look death in the face calm and unafraid, and to confess with certainty his faith in the resurrection of the body and the life everlasting.

The third day! Small wonder the Church has ever since celebrated it as the great weekly festival of Christian praise when its members meet together to worship the living Lord and to remember him in the breaking of bread. For us, what the apostle calls here the *third* day is the *first* day, the Lord's day, and every Sunday is a 'little Easter' when we raise to God our alleluias.

On the third morn he rose again,
Glorious in majesty to reign,
O let us swell the joyful strain:
Alleluia!

EASTER

The first Easter communion

Luke 24.30 (NEB) '*When he had sat down with them at table, he took bread and said the blessing; he broke the bread, and offered it to them.*'

Have you ever come across that rubric in the Prayer Book which says, 'Note, that every parishioner shall communicate at least three times in the year, of which Easter to be one'? The rubric is of interest because it reflects a longstanding Christian tradition, that Easter communion should be regarded as an obligation on the part of every church member.

Is that merely a medieval tradition? How far back does it go? When did Easter communion begin? The answer is that the first Easter communion (or something remarkably like it) took place at Emmaus on the day of the Lord's resurrection when he shared an evening meal with two of his followers at Emmaus and 'was known to them in the breaking of bread'. He himself, the risen Lord, was the host, presiding at the table. The guests or worshippers were two obscure, unknown disciples—just ordinary Christians like ourselves. The place was a humble village home where these two lived. There it was that Jesus 'took bread and said the blessing, broke the bread, and offered it to them'.

Let me ask you to note some other features of that first Easter communion, because what happened then is typical of what every communion service should be like.

1. *At the first Easter communion the breaking of bread was preceded by the breaking of the Word*

The sacrament was closely linked with the scriptures. Or to put it more simply still, and in more modern terms, there was a sermon before communion and in close connection with it.

When was the sermon preached? On the road, in the course of the seven-mile walk from Jerusalem to Emmaus, when 'beginning with Moses and all the prophets, Jesus interpreted to them in all the scriptures the things concerning himself'. That must have been one of the most remarkable sermons ever preached, even though the 'congregation' numbered only two. It was a sermon firmly based on scripture and full of Christ—the crucified and glorified Messiah. Small wonder that later on the two disciples confessed to one another, 'Did not our hearts burn within us while he talked to us on the road, while he opened to us the scriptures?'

Preaching does warm the heart as well as inform the mind when it is like that—Bible-based and Christ-centred. I admit, there is a kind of preaching which leaves me cold: preaching without any genuine scriptural content and with little or nothing to say about the Lord Jesus himself. However, the point I am making now is simply this, that sermon and sacrament belong together. Here is an important principle which was recovered for the Church at the time of the Reformation and which today happily is receiving fresh attention. The principle goes right back to the beginning. Before Jesus broke bread with his disciples at Emmaus he had already opened to them the scriptures and fed them with the Word.

2. *At the first Easter communion the disciples knew the presence of the risen Lord*

Something wonderful happened when he broke the bread and gave it to them. 'Their eyes were opened and they recognised him; and he vanished from their sight.' Earlier on, you will recall, they had failed to recognise him (see verse 16). Now they knew him; and he was known to them in the breaking of bread.

It was a memorable experience for these two disciples. There at the Lord's table they met with the Lord. They were conscious of his living presence and power. The doubts that had haunted their minds before were now dissolved. Their faith was restored. They knew without a shadow of doubt that Jesus was alive—their victorious Saviour and Lord.

Is that what the Lord's supper does for us? Does it help to make Jesus come alive for us? Does it make his presence real? Does it enable us to feed on him in our hearts by faith with thanksgiving? The words of a little known hymn by James Montgomery should be our constant prayer at communion:

> Be known to us in breaking bread,
> But do not then depart;
> Saviour, abide with us, and spread
> Thy table in our heart.
>
> There sup with us in love divine:
> Thy body and thy blood,
> That living bread, that heavenly wine,
> Be our immortal food,

3. *At the first Easter communion worship was followed by witness*

Those two disciples rose from the table conscious of a new purpose, charged with a sense of mission. Christ was alive! This was now their burning conviction and they must tell the good news to others. They could not keep it to themselves. So the first thing they did was to hurry back to Jerusalem, where they found the rest of their company and shared with them their glowing experience (verses 33–35).

Worship and witness belong together. The one is the preparation for the other. Martin Parsons tells of a church building where over the chancel arch, facing the nave, are the words of the Great Invitation: 'Come unto me, all ye that labour and are heavy laden, and I will give you rest.' Every worshipper as he goes up to receive communion is able to read and rejoice in that invitation. Then, as he leaves the Lord's table and returns to his place, he sees on the chancel side of the arch the words of the Great Commission: 'Go ye into all the world, and preach the gospel to every creature.' We come to the Lord's supper to find refreshment. We go from it to serve him better in the world.

EASTER

A glorious impossibility

Acts 2.24 '*It was not possible for him to be held by it.*'

'It's quite impossible!' That's the general reaction to the story of our Lord's resurrection on the part of the unbeliever, be he atheist, agnostic, humanist, or whatever. And of course he has reason on his side. And science too. And history as well. After all, it's a simple fact: dead men don't come back to life—not those who are well and truly dead. So on general grounds whatever happened in the case of Jesus, it's utterly impossible to believe that he rose from the dead.

Yet in the words of my text we have the apostle Peter saying just the opposite. He is preaching in Jerusalem on the feast of Pentecost, only a few weeks after the crucifixion. He boldly declares that Jesus had been rejected by the Jews and killed by the hands of lawless men; then he adds, 'But God raised him up, having loosed the pangs of death, because *it was not possible for him to be held by it.*'

1. *The mastery of death*

Here is a glorious impossibility. There are those, as I have said, who find the resurrection of Jesus quite incredible. It was impossible, they say, for him to rise from the dead. What the apostle affirms is that it was impossible for him *not* to rise! The impossibility consists not in his rising from the dead but in his being held captive by death.

It *was* possible for Jesus to die. The New Testament has no doubt about the reality of his death because it has no doubt about the reality of his manhood. When he took upon him our human nature he became true man, subject to all the vicissitudes of this mortal life. His death was evidence of that fact.

But the New Testament, while it declares that it was possible for Jesus to die, and that he really did die, states with equal certainty that it was quite impossible for him to remain dead—to be subject to the tyranny of death. This is the implication of the Greek word rendered *held*. The verb means to master. It was not possible for Jesus to be mastered by death. No! He was the Master of death.

2. *The key to the resurrection*

Here is the ultimate argument for the resurrection, if argument is needed. All kinds of arguments can of course be produced, and all have some value. But in the end *the key to the resurrection is the person of Jesus Christ himself.*

'It was not possible for *him* to be held by *it*.' Let me ask you to look carefully at those two little pronouns. They are both significant. The *he* is the Lord Jesus Christ. The *it* is the great enemy of man—Death. Here in dramatic fashion these two mighty opposing forces, Christ and Death, are brought face to face. And the victory lies not on the side of Death but of Christ.

The fact is, it was not possible that Christ, being what he is, should be held captive by death, considering what death is.

For who is Jesus Christ? He is the eternal Son of God. He is the sinless Son of Man. Clearly then he is unique—the God-Man, perfect alike in his deity and his humanity. And equally clearly death had no claim upon him, no power over him, no place in his life.

For again, what is death? The answer of the Bible is that

death, like sin, is a foreign element in human life. Indeed, death is that separation between man and God which is the penalty of sin. That is why Paul calls death the 'wages' of sin: the due reward which sin pays to its servants. But Jesus was not the servant of sin. He was without sin and therefore sin had no right to touch him. Nevertheless he died, as we have admitted. Why? Because he voluntarily identified himself with the sin of man, assumed responsibility for it, and on the cross he paid its penalty by *death*—that death which involves separation from God.

3. *The victory of the cross*

What is the outcome? Having paid the penalty on man's behalf, Christ has made an end of sin. He has won the victory over sin and, as a result, over death as well. As St Paul puts it, death has been robbed of its sting, for the sting of death is sin.

Let us be quite sure that the cross is Christ's victory, not his defeat. And the resurrection is the demonstration of that victory, the divine vindication of the triumph Christ achieved on Calvary for man's redemption.

R. C. Moberly wrote: 'Easter is the interpretation of Good Friday. The significance of the cross is revealed in the resurrection. The resurrection is not so much a mere sequel to the cross, or a reversal of the cross, or a subsequent reward because of the endurance of the cross. Rather, it is a revealing of what the cross already was.'

That is why it was not possible for Jesus to be imprisoned by the tyrant death. Having by his passion won the victory over sin, he had at the same time robbed death of all its power.

Has all this any relevance for our modern world? Most certainly! For multitudes today life is a hopeless, meaningless struggle and death is the final, inevitable word. They can see no sense of purpose in or beyond this world, and so they abandon themselves to the passing pleasures of the moment. 'Let us eat and drink, for tomorrow we die.' That is logical enough—if death is really the end.

But death is not the end! Death is vanquished. Christ has

conquered it. As the ancient fathers delighted to affirm, the death of Jesus is 'the death of death'. And his glorious resurrection not only attests and demonstrates his victory. It also brings his living presence into the lives of his people *now*. As Dr T. R. Glover said, 'The gospels are not four, but ten thousand times ten thousand, and thousands of thousands, and the last word of every one of them is, Lo, I am with you always, even unto the end of the world.'

EASTER

What men make of the resurrection

> Acts 17.32–34 '*When they heard of the resurrection of the dead, some mocked; but others said, "We will hear you again about this." So Paul went out from among them. But some men joined him and believed.*'

Paul was on a visit to Athens, the intellectual centre of the world of his day, the home of Greek philosophy. He had come there on his second missionary journey, about the year AD 50, preaching (as Luke tells us) 'Jesus and the resurrection'. This had puzzled the local religious experts and he had been invited to expound his message to their supreme court, the Areopagus. 'May we know', they asked, 'what this new teaching is which you present?'

So we see the apostle standing before these Athenian philosophers and proclaiming to them the gospel of Christ. As he nears the end of his address, he speaks in solemn terms of the judgement of mankind which God has committed to Jesus Christ; and of this fact, Paul asserts, God 'has given assurance to all men *by raising him from the dead*'.

What was the result? Luke mentions a threefold reaction to the preaching of the resurrection of Jesus. He says some mocked; other hesitated, as though uncertain what to do; while yet others accepted the message and joined the apostle.

It's much the same today. If we ask, What do men make of the resurrection? the answer is that there are still the scoffers, the doubters, and the believers.

1. *The scoffers*

When they heard of the resurrection of Christ, 'some mocked'. This was to be expected in a place like Athens. The god Apollo is claimed to have said, when that very court of the Areopagus was founded, 'Once a man dies and the earth drinks up his blood, there is no resurrection'. It's hardly surprising then that there were those who dismissed what Paul said as a piece of fantastic nonsense. To these wise men of Athens the idea of Jesus rising from the dead was so out of harmony with their philosophy that they simply ridiculed the whole thing. They just laughed. They treated it as a big joke.

There are those today who adopt much the same attitude. They scoff at Christianity and regard it as incredulous just because of its supernatural claims and character. 'Miracles are unscientific', they say. 'No rational person believes in them nowadays. As for the resurrection of Jesus—well, everybody knows that dead men don't rise again.'

We have heard all this before and I am not particularly concerned with the scoffers, whether ancient or modern. I would simply offer two observations. *First*, the Athenian philosophers mocked at the resurrection without any attempt to examine the facts or investigate the subject. And the same is often true of modern scoffers; whereas the evidence for Christ's resurrection is so powerful that it cannot simply be laughed away. *Second*, mocking at a fact doesn't alter the fact. It merely magnifies the folly of the scoffers. When Copernicus asserted that the earth went round the sun and not vice versa—some mocked! But the fact remained and was quite unaffected by their jeers.

2. *The doubters*

Not all those who heard Paul mocked. Some said, 'We will hear you again about this.' It is possible of course that those who spoke like that were simply procrastinating or politely declining to pursue the subject further. I venture to think otherwise. I believe these people had been genuinely impressed by what they heard: impressed, but not yet convinced. They were hesitant to commit themselves without learning more and asking certain questions, and so clearing up their doubts.

I believe there are many nowadays in much the same position. There is much in the claims of Christianity which attracts them, but they are hesitant and questioning when it comes to the resurrection of our Lord. For example, there are those who find difficulties in the gospel records of the event. At certain points, they say, those records seem to be inconsistent, and even contradictory: can they therefore be trustworthy? What they fail to see is that the very differences bear witness to the *independence* of the four records, and that this independence adds considerably to the value of their testimony; for while there is variety of detail, there is complete unanimity with regard to the central fact: that on the third day the grave was empty and that the risen Lord appeared to his disciples and convinced them that he was alive.

The doubts of others arise from rationalistic 'explanations' of the empty tomb. Perhaps someone stole the body of Jesus? Perhaps the women went to the wrong tomb? Perhaps the disciples suffered from hallucinations? And so on. None of these ideas will hold water, as a moment's thought will show. Those who have honest doubts should drag them out into the open and do a little honest thinking. They will find the New Testament evidence is clear, consistent and convincing.

3. *The believers*

Paul's witness in Athens was not a failure. 'Some men joined him and believed, among them Dionysius the Areopagite and a woman named Damaris and others with them.' Yes, these *believed*—as I trust we do. But that raises a question. What does it mean to believe in the resurrection of Jesus Christ?

For one thing, it does not merely mean to accept the historical truth that Christ rose from the dead. It means to commit yourself to him in complete trust and confidence as your living Lord. Belief in the resurrection has to do not only with a *fact* but with a *person*.

And one other thing. Our belief in the resurrection rests on more than intellectual conviction. It rests also on spiritual experience and what Christ means to us in daily life. The most convincing and compelling argument for the truth of the Easter story is given by St Paul when he says, 'It is no longer I who live, but Christ who lives in me.' And the result will be, inevitably, a life of service for others in the name and strength of the risen Lord.

ASCENSION

Christ in majesty

Acts 1.9 '*He was lifted up, and a cloud took him out of their sight.*'

It's natural enough in this scientific age that people should be more interested in what actually *happened* at the ascension of Jesus than in what it all *means*. 'He was lifted up', says the New Testament account. Well, was he? Did he really go *up*? If so, where did he go to? Into 'heaven'? But where is heaven? The Russian cosmonaut, Gherman Titov, reported laconically that he saw 'no signs of God in outer space.' Of course not. Titov was an atheist and people who are spiritually blind can't see heavenly things. Jesus himself said so: 'Unless a man is born again he cannot see the kingdom of God.'

The point is that when the New Testament affirms that Jesus 'was lifted up and a cloud took him out of their sight' it is dealing with spiritual truth, not with scientific dogma. It is concerned with the world of ultimate reality which lies beyond the present order of time and space. That spiritual world can only be represented to us in picture language, in forms and images which we can understand. So in the ascension story we must remember that the 'cloud' is a symbol of God's Glory or Presence, and that 'heaven' represents his transcendence—his majesty and power.

With that in mind, we can take a look at some of the particular aspects of the New Testament portrait of the ascended Christ.

1. *Christ the Conqueror*

The first and most dramatic picture with which the ascension confronts us is that of *Christus Victor*—the conquering Christ, triumphant in glory. 'God has highly exalted him and bestowed on him the name which is above every name, that at the name of Jesus every knee should bow.'

In half a dozen places the New Testament speaks of Jesus in his victorious status as being 'seated on the right hand of God'. What does that mean? It is an expression borrowed from the Old Testament; and as Dr Norman Snaith remarks, 'To sit at the right hand of God is, from Psalm 110 onwards, the privilege of the triumphant Messiah. This is the meaning here. When his earthly life was completed, Jesus returned to his high estate, and he returned as Conqueror. That which he had come to earth to do, he had accomplished, and he had accomplished it triumphantly.'

The ascension bears witness to Christ's finished work, his victorious redemption, his conquest of the two greatest enemies of mankind—sin and death.

2. *Christ the King*

The Conqueror is also the King. The exalted Christ is the reigning Christ. As the writer to the Hebrews says, 'We see Jesus, who for a short while was made lower than the angels, crowned now with glory and honour because he suffered death.'

The attention of any visitor to Coventry cathedral is inevitably caught first by Graham Sutherland's vast tapestry which hangs behind the high altar and takes the place of reredos and east window. Whether or not he actually likes it as a work of art, he can scarcely fail to be impressed by the striking design and the rich colours. Its title? 'Christ in Glory.' And that is the title we might well give to the ascension. It is essentially the festival of Christ the King. It symbolises his sovereignty: not only over his Church but over the whole of creation. The Lamb is on the throne. Nothing so sustains our faith in dark and difficult times as the assurance that our Lord reigns, exalted as head of the new humanity, and that all authority is his both in heaven and on earth.

3. *Christ the Intercessor*

A third picture is that of Christ as the Intercessor, our Advocate with the Father, who appears before the presence of God for us. The ascension is closely linked not only with his kingship but also with his priesthood.

Here again we are in the realm of symbolical thought, and we can only express that thought in symbolical language. But the meaning is unmistakable. Once more it is the writer of the letter to the Hebrews who develops this idea most fully. He insists that in virtue of his one perfect sacrifice for sin Christ has entered heaven as the great High Priest of his people and that now 'he is able for all time to save those who draw near to God through him, since he always lives to make intercession for them.'

Perhaps we find it hard to take in what is meant by Christ's intercession; but at least we can see in it the emblem of his abiding love for his Church on earth and the assurance of the eternal efficacy of his saving work. Christ lives in the glory of the Father as the undying, unfailing, unforgetting Friend and Saviour of mankind.

4. *Christ the Forerunner*

One final thing. The Bible portrait of Christ in majesty brings us a fresh assurance of our own eternal destiny. For when he returned to the Father our Lord entered heaven as the 'Forerunner' of his people. That actual expression is found in Hebrews (6.20), and Bishop Westcott points out that the

Greek word (*prodromos*) was used especially of troops who were sent on in advance of the main army to seek out the way and to make ready for the rest to follow. This is the meaning of the word here. The Lord has gone on ahead to prepare a place for us, and his ascension is the pledge that we at last shall follow where he has gone. This is the thought of the Ascensiontide collect, which asks that God may 'exalt us unto the same place whither our Saviour Christ is gone before'.

ASCENSION

Christ's finished work and the Church's unfinished mission

Mark 16.19, 20 '*The Lord Jesus, after he had spoken to them, was taken up into heaven, and sat down at the right hand of God. And they went forth and preached everywhere, while the Lord worked with them and confirmed the message by the signs that attended it.*'

These two verses, which round off St Mark's gospel in its so-called 'longer ending', present two contrasting pictures of Christ and his Church. We see Christ in heaven, and the Church on earth; and again, we see Christ 'sitting down', and the Church 'going forth'. These pictures suggest my subject for today: the finished work of Christ and the unfinished mission of the Church.

1. *Christ's finished work*

The ascension of our Lord has several meanings for us, but for the disciples at the time it had one quite immediate meaning. It made clear to them in a decisive way that his ministry on earth had reached its end.

The actual story of the ascension, related in the first chapter of Acts, is best looked upon as the Lord's last resurrection appearance to his apostles. That appearance was accompanied by a miraculous sign or symbol which indicated to them that his mission in the world was completed, that he was returning to the glory of the Father, and that they would see him in visible form no more. All he had come into the world to do as the incarnate Son he had achieved, by his life and death and resurrection; now therefore he withdrew his visible presence from earth in order to continue his ministry in heaven.

When Christ came into the world his prayer was, 'Lo, I have come to do thy will, O God'. When he left the world it was, 'I have finished the work which thou gavest me to do'. Then what next? 'He was taken up into heaven, and sat down at the right hand of God.' The language of course is pictorial, for it is only in such terms that we can envisage our Lord's heavenly state; but the picture is unmistakably clear and bears witness to the glory of a completed task.

He sat down at the right hand of God. The words have found their way into the Apostles' Creed in the clause dealing with the ascension. They echo the opening verse of Psalm 110—that psalm which has the distinction of being more often quoted in the New Testament than any other Old Testament passage. The psalm as a whole is a triumphant ode describing in vivid and dramatic language (1) the Messiah's conquest of his foes as he leads his host out to battle, (2) his kingly rule as he sits upon the throne of God and wields his sceptre, and (3) his mediatorial role as he exercises his royal priesthood—'a priest for ever after the order of Melchizedek'.

In terms like these we may contemplate the meaning of our Lord's ascension into heaven. The total picture is one of glory, triumph, achievement. In his striking hymn of the ascension, Bishop Christopher Wordsworth expressed it thus:

Who is this who comes in glory,
With the trump of jubilee?
Lord of battles, God of armies,
He has gained the victory;
He who on the cross did suffer,
He who from the grave arose,

He has vanquished sin and Satan,
He by death has spoiled his foes.

2. *The Church's unfinished mission*

'They went forth and preached everywhere, while the Lord worked with them and confirmed the message by the signs that attended it.' Here is the other side of the story—the earthly side. Christ's mission was completed. The Church's mission was just beginning. They went out into the world in obedience to the Lord's command to be his witnesses, to preach the good news to the whole creation, to make disciples for him from all nations.

That was their task then. It is our task still, the task of the whole Church; for before he left the world to return to the Father the Lord constituted his entire Church into a society for the propagation of the gospel—and the Church is only truly *his* Church when it is engaged in mission.

The mission is a continuing thing, for the task is not yet complete. That is why we in our day have our part to play, everyone of us. It's not an easy job: the devil sees to that! But our comfort is that we do not go it alone, any more than did those first disciples. As they went forth to their witness '*the Lord worked with them*'. How did he work with them? In the power of his Spirit. We must never forget that the ascent of God the Son was followed by the descent of God the Spirit. The missionary Church is a pentecostal Church. Christ never envisaged it otherwise. 'Lo, I am with you always' was his last word to those he sent.

The Church is the Body of Christ, and Christ is the Head of the Body. The Head is in heaven—exalted, triumphant, reigning. The Body is on earth—fighting, witnessing, suffering. But the Body is in vital union with the Head, under his direction and control, and it is through the instrumentality of his Body that the Head carries on his work in the world and extends his empire over the lives of men.

'Now *you* are the body of Christ and individually members of it.'

WHITSUN

The Spirit-filled community

I Corinthians 12.13 *'By one Spirit we were all baptized into one body—Jews or Greeks, slaves or free—and all were made to drink of one Spirit.'*

What is the Church? Where is it to be found? How is it to be identified?

Doubtless all sorts of answers could be given to those questions, just because the Church has so many different aspects and can be described in a variety of ways. But one thing is certain. Any attempt to define the Church which leaves out the Holy Spirit cannot be regarded as satisfactory. That is why the questions I have asked are good ones for us to think about on the feast of Pentecost.

1. *Institutional religion*

Some few years ago Bishop Lesslie Newbigin wrote a particularly fine book about the Church called *The Household of God*. Among other things it contains an arresting chapter entitled 'The Community of the Holy Spirit', in which he examines the relation of the Spirit to the Church in the light of New Testament teaching. At the outset of the chapter he points out that if from this particular angle we would answer the question, 'Where is the Church?' we must ask another question: 'Where is the Holy Spirit recognisably present with power?' For as he says a bit later on, the Holy Spirit may be the last article of the creed, but in the New Testament the Spirit is the first fact of Christian experience.

Here is something we must take note of. There is a growing impatience today with institutional religion. Young people in particular have lost faith in the Church as a piece of ecclesiastical machinery—and rightly so. It's all very proper to sing 'Like a mighty army moves the Church of God', but nobody feels like singing 'Like a mighty engine moves the Church of God'!

We must rise above the institutional level. There is no future in denominational Christianity. It's useless to go on attaching human labels to the Church of God, as though it were a man-made thing. You will remember that there were those in the church at Corinth who did so and variously claimed 'I am of Paul', 'I am of Apollos', and so on. Shame on us, we have been inclined to talk in that way too: to say 'I am of Luther' (Lutherans), 'I am of Calvin' (Calvinists), 'I am of Wesley' (Wesleyans).

All such thinking reflects a wretchedly low view of the Church. It is time we got a better and bigger view, the sort of view the apostle Paul gives us in our text: 'By one Spirit we were all baptised into one body, and were all made to drink of one Spirit.'

2. *The Spirit-filled Body*

Paul is thinking of the Church as the one Body of Christ and of Christians as the different 'members' of the Body—its organs and limbs. How do we become members of the one Body? The apostle's answer is, 'By the one Spirit'. He says: 'By one Spirit we were all baptised into one body.' As Christians, he means, we have not only been baptised with water, the outward and visible sign. We have also been baptised with the Spirit—'immersed' in the Spirit, so to speak—and so made living members of Christ's Body. Then he uses another figure: 'we were all made to drink of the one Spirit'. He means that as Christians we have all received the Spirit within us and are now filled, imbued, saturated with the Spirit.

Christian baptism is not just water-baptism, the sort of thing administered by John the Baptist. John himself made that clear. He spoke of the difference between his ministry and that of Christ. 'I have baptised you with water,' he said; 'but he will baptise you with the Holy Spirit.'

I am convinced that we ought to place far more stress than we do upon the truth that it is the presence of the Holy Spirit that constitutes the living Church and gives it validity. Where the Spirit of Christ is, there the Body of Christ is. Equally, where the Spirit of Christ is not, there the Body of Christ is not. Or at any rate, it is no more than a dead body.

3. *Dynamic Christianity*

Here we have a far more dynamic approach to the question, Where is the Church? than the static view offered by traditional Christianity, whether Catholic or Protestant. In trying to identify the true Church the Catholic side magnifies the apostolic succession, while the Protestant side makes much of the apostolic faith. Properly understood, both are important; yet in the last resort neither is decisive for the life of the Church. What *is* decisive is the answer given to the question put to the converts at Ephesus: 'Did you receive the Holy Spirit when you believed?'

Let me quote Bishop Newbigin once again: 'The church lives neither by her faithfulness to her message nor by her abiding in one fellowship with the apostles; she lives by the living power of the Spirit of God.' Yes, and without that living power the most impeccable orders of ministry or the most orthodox brand of faith is of little account.

Well, what does this mean for ourselves? It means, surely, that we ought not to be content with the low spiritual level to which in general we have become accustomed as Christian people. Rather, we should be seeking a more dynamic experience of the saving power of Christ, a deeper unity of the Spirit in our relations with our fellow-Christians, a new quality of church life which will make manifest that God is among us of a truth.

When the Church is filled with the Spirit the world will know it, just as truly as it knew it on the day of Pentecost. The evidence now may well be different from what it was then. We need not expect the same spectacular 'spiritual gifts' which marked the life of the early Church and which some today are all too anxious to cultivate—or maybe imitate. Nevertheless the evidence will not be lacking. A tree is known by its fruit, as Jesus insisted. And fruit can be seen and tasted. What is the fruit borne by a Spirit-filled Church? Miracles? Healings? Tongues? No. 'The fruit of the Spirit is love, joy, peace. . . .'

WHITSUN

Living on the right side of Pentecost

Acts 2.1, 4 '*When the day of Pentecost had come . . . they were all filled with the Holy Spirit.*'

What a difference it makes when a Church is living on the right side of Pentecost! If you want to know how great the difference is, I invite you to compare the picture of our Lord's disciples in the first chapter of Acts, before the day of Pentecost, and the picture of them in the second chapter, when the Spirit had come.

There could scarcely be a more striking contrast.

1. *The Church before Pentecost*

Look for a moment at the picture of the Church in Acts 1. The early part of the chapter tells of how during the great forty days after Easter the risen Lord 'showed himself alive' to his disciples and spoke to them about the kingdom of God. He also made clear to them their own responsible role in the programme of the kingdom. 'You shall receive power', he promised, 'when the Holy Spirit has come upon you: and you shall be my witnesses in Jerusalem and in all Judea and Samaria and to the end of the earth.'

Then the Lord was taken from them in visible presence and they returned from the mount of Olives to Jerusalem and assembled in the upper room where they were staying—to wait and to pray.

We see them there: a congregation or 'Church' of about 120, all devoted disciples of Jesus Christ, all obedient to his word. Yet quite obviously something is wanting. For what sort of a Church is this? What do we see?

. . . a Church shut in from the world, in retreat from the world, not going out into the world to bear witness to Christ.

. . . a waiting Church: a Church waiting for something to

happen instead of taking action in Christ's name to make things happen.

. . . a Church bereft of the presence of the Lord, orphaned, impoverished, unready, a Church without spiritual power.

. . . a praying Church indeed (and we must not forget that) but a Church whose prayers had not yet been answered.

. . . a Church preoccupied with its own affairs rather than with the needs of others: a Church busily concerned about the apostolic succession but as yet achieving no apostolic success.

It is a picture of a Church living on the wrong side of Pentecost. A disappointing picture indeed.

2. *The Church after Pentecost*

Then something happened which changed the whole situation. What happened? Pentecost! The wind of God swept through the Church. The fire fell from heaven upon the disciples. This is how the story goes:

> When the day of Pentecost had come, they were all together in one place. And suddenly a sound came from heaven like the rush of a mighty wind, and it filled all the house where they were sitting. And there appeared to them tongues as of fire, distributed and resting on each one of them. And they were all filled with the Holy Spirit and began to speak in other tongues, as the Spirit gave them utterance.

Here is a very different picture from that given in the previous section. It's a picture of a Church living on the right side of Pentecost, a Church filled with the Spirit—the Spirit of Christ. For when the Spirit came, it was just as though the Lord Jesus himself were with his people again as in the days of old, manifesting his presence in their midst.

The first activity of these Spirit-filled men and women was that they began to *speak*. The Church was no longer silent. How could it be when the Spirit came upon them like *tongues of fire*? The tongue is the organ of speech. It is because I have a tongue in my head that I am able to talk to you now. So when the Spirit manifested himself on the day of Pentecost.

> He came in tongues of living flame,
> To teach, convince, subdue.

A Church living on the right side of Pentecost is a confessional Church, bearing witness to the faith of Christ and sharing his good news with others. The greater part of this second chapter of Acts is taken up with the sermon preached that same day by the apostle Peter, as he boldly set forth the claims of the crucified and risen Jesus as both Lord and Christ. The result: 'those who received his word were baptised, and there were added that day about three thousand souls.'

The last part of the chapter presents an impressive picture of corporate Christianity. Warmed by the fire of the Spirit, the Church discovers the meaning of fellowship. Look at the picture:

> They devoted themselves to the apostles' teaching and fellowship, to the breaking of bread and the prayers.... And all who believed were together and had all things in common.... And day by day, attending the temple together and breaking bread in their homes, they partook of food with glad and generous hearts, praising God and having favour with all the people.

Here is another characteristic of a Church living on the right side of Pentecost. It knows something of the fellowship of the Spirit. 'All that believed were together.' Do we know the meaning of that?

Two Christians were discussing their respective churches.

'How are things in your church?' one asked the other.

'We're all united', was the reply. 'We're all frozen together.'

The fire of Pentecost can thaw our cold hearts and *weld* us together, so that every Church becomes a true community of the Spirit. That is why we need to pray:

> Come, Holy Ghost, our souls inspire,
> And lighten with *celestial fire*.

Part Two. Holy Days

ST ANDREW

A man with a mission

John 1.42 '*He brought him to Jesus.*'

What is the greatest service that one man can do another? According to Archbishop William Temple is it what Andrew did for his brother Simon Peter: 'he brought him to Jesus.' Should we ever have heard of Simon Peter if Andrew had not done that? And in that case how extraordinarily different the history of the Christian Church might have been! A Church without Peter? Impossible, some would say. And even if we're not prepared to go quite as far as that, we would surely agree that Andrew did a magnificent job that day—not only for Peter but for the whole Church—when 'he brought him to Jesus'.

But now a question arises. How was Andrew himself brought to our Lord? We must go back a bit in the story to find out.

1. *How Andrew found Christ*

As far as Andrew was concerned, it all began with the preaching of John the Baptist. Andrew had been attracted by his preaching and had become one of his disciples. Then one day, along with another disciple, he was standing with the Baptist when Jesus passed by. Looking at him, and perhaps pointing towards him, John cried, 'Behold , the Lamb of God!' At once the two disciples left their old master and followed Jesus and spent the rest of the day in his company.

What passed between Andrew and Jesus that day is not

related. Perhaps Andrew felt it was of too personal a character to put on record. But we may be sure that he never forgot that interview, that face-to-face encounter with Jesus. It changed the whole current of his life. It gave to his life a new dimension, a new depth. And, humanly speaking, he owed it all to John, that self-effacing man who was content to describe himself as 'a voice crying in the wilderness' and whose task was to 'prepare the way of the Lord'. John made full proof of his ministry that day when he pointed Andrew to Jesus. It was the beginning of great things for the Church of Christ.

2. *How Andrew won his brother for Christ*

If we do not know what Jesus said to Andrew, or what Andrew said to Jesus, when they thus met, we do know the outcome of that memorable encounter. Andrew, we are told, 'first found his brother Simon, and said to him, "We have found the Messiah!"' It was such a tremendous discovery that Andrew felt he could not keep it to himself. He must share the good news, and the one with whom he wanted to share it first of all was his own brother. Without wasting any time or giving Simon a chance to argue or protest, he simply told him what he had found, and then—'he brought him to Jesus'.

Because of what he did Andrew has earned the title of the first Christian missionary, and it is a title he well deserves. Indeed it is in a missionary capacity that he is now remembered and honoured in the Church. For what is a missionary? Not simply a prophet or teacher or social reformer, but one who passes on the good news of Jesus Christ and so seeks to bring others to him. And this is evangelism, at least in the New Testament sense.

'He brought him to Jesus.' The one he brought was his own brother; and it's surely worth noting that for Andrew missionary work began at home. He was a missionary in that place where it is most difficult for us to bear our witness—in the family circle. But let us not forget that for Andrew missionary work did not stop there. Later on in this same gospel (chapter 12) we find him introducing some Greek inquirers—that is, Gentiles—to Jesus.

All this shows clearly enough the kind of man Andrew was. He was not a born leader like his brother Simon, nor was he destined to fulfil a prominent role in the later life of the Church (the Acts of the Apostles tells us nothing about his work). But clearly he was a friendly, approachable man, a man who worked in the background and knew how to get on with people; and above all, a man with a concern for others, a man with a mission, and a man who became, at the call of Jesus, a fisher of men (see today's gospel).

APPLICATION

The customary application of the 'message' of St Andrew's Day is an urgent appeal to support the missionary work of the Church overseas. This is excellent and most important. But ought we not to face a more personal application? Are not we ourselves under an obligation to do for others what Andrew did for Peter when he brought him to Jesus? Does not Christ challenge us in the same terms, 'Follow me, and I will make you fishers of men'? It's not an easy task, admittedly; but it's a task in which we can all have our share by the prayers we offer, the faith we exercise, the concern we express, the example we set, the life we live and the words we speak. In ways such as these each one of us is 'called to be an apostle'.

ST THOMAS

A misunderstood man

John 20.28 '*Thomas answered him, "My Lord and my God!"*'

One way or another, Thomas has had a pretty raw deal at the hands of preachers and commentators. He is possibly the most misunderstood man in the Bible. It is all too easy to magnify his faults and ignore his virtues. This is all the more so since we are told comparatively little about him, and all that we are told is found in St John's gospel (in the other gospels he is no more than a name). What then are the facts? There are three passages to engage our attention and from them a fairly clear picture of this man emerges.

1. *A courageous man*

The first passage is in chapter 11 in connection with the death of Lazarus. Jesus alarmed the disciples by announcing that he was going to Bethany in Judaea to raise Lazarus. Judaea was hostile to Jesus. The authorities in Jerusalem were plotting to kill him. To go to Judaea at such a time seemed disastrous and perhaps some of the disciples hesitated to accompany him. But then Thomas spoke up and said, 'Let us also go, that we may die with him' (verse 16).

Thomas doubtless saw, as clearly as the rest, that the way ahead was fraught with danger, but as far as he was concerned there was no question of turning back and being a deserter. If Jesus was set on going to Jerusalem, he would go too, whatever the cost. If Jesus was prepared to face death, he would also face it, along with his Lord. 'Let us also go, that we may die with him'—these are the words of a brave man, a man of heroic mould, determined to be faithful unto death.

2. *An honest man*

It was my privilege many years ago to listen to a Bible lecture about Thomas given by Dr G. Campbell Morgan at Westminster Chapel, London. The lecture threw new light on the character of this man, as far as I was concerned. One of the points which Dr Morgan brought out was Thomas's absolute honesty. As he said, Thomas was not the kind of man who would profess approbation and understanding of something that baffled him. He would not affect a faith he did not possess.

This comes out in the well-known passage in chapter 14

where Jesus told the disciples he was going to prepare a place for them, and added, 'Where I am going you know, and the way you know'. At once Thomas blurted out, 'Lord, we do not know where you are going! How can we know the way?' It was a bold thing for Thomas to do, to contradict his Master; but, honest man as he was, he felt he must speak the truth. And his protest brought back from the Lord the wonderful answer, 'I am the way, and the truth, and the life; no one comes to the Father but by me.'

This is the sort of man Thomas was—a magnificently honest man. There was nothing of the humbug about him. He couldn't bear any sort of pretence. And here surely he has something to teach us in our church life. Let's try to be a bit more honest with each other as well as with the Lord. Let's get rid of all pretence in our religious talk, in our prayers, in our worship, in our dealings with people; and let's remember that it *is* possible to speak the truth in love.

3. *A convinced man*

We come now to the passage which forms the gospel for the feast of St Thomas (John 20.24–31). The previous verses tell of the Lord's appearance to the disciples in his risen power on the evening of the first Easter day. 'But Thomas was not with them when Jesus came', says the evangelist. Later Thomas rejoined them but stubbornly refused to believe their account of how they had seen the Lord. 'Unless I see in his hands the print of the nails, and place my finger in the mark of the nails, and place my hand in his side, I will not believe.' Here is doubting Thomas with a vengeance!

Why did he take up this attitude? To answer that question we must, I think, ask another. *Why had he not been with the other disciples when Jesus appeared to them*? Was it not, in all probability, because the experience of Good Friday had been too much for him? He had seen Jesus crucified, his hands nailed, his side pierced, and hope had died within him. He was plunged into utter spiritual darkness. Such was the grief and agony and horror through which he passed that he felt he must get away from everyone and brood in solitude over what had happened. That was the big mistake he made. If only he had stayed within the fellowship of the disciples! And if only he had believed what they told him! But he couldn't force himself to believe. He was too honest to pretend. He was seeking certainty. He must be *sure* Jesus was alive—the same Jesus who had been crucified. Hence his demand: 'Unless I see . . .'

The risen Lord met his demand. When a week later he appeared again to the disciples Thomas was with them, and he invited Thomas to touch the nail-prints and the wounded side. But Thomas was already convinced and made the great confession, 'My Lord and my God!' It was at once an affirmation of faith, an act of worship, and a cry of surrender.

Thomas was a convinced man. He was convinced in the end not by argument or reasoning but (as Dr William Barclay has put it) 'through firsthand experience of the power and presence of Jesus Christ'. We may share his conviction and enjoy the same experience as we claim for ourselves Jesus' last beatitude: 'Blessed are those who have not seen and yet believe' (verse 29).

ST STEPHEN

Christ's witness

Acts 6.5 '*They chose Stephen, a man of faith and of the Holy Spirit.*'

Everybody knows that 'Good King Wenceslas looked out on the Feast of Stephen', but it's fairly safe to assume that not everybody knows what the Feast of Stephen is all about. The fact that the festival falls immediately after Christmas—on Boxing day—is enough to ensure that it is largely neglected and ignored, even by regular church people.

This is a thousand pities, for Stephen is a name to be honoured in the Church as the first Christian martyr. It is well to remember in that connection that our word 'martyr' comes directly from the Greek *martus*, meaning a witness. So a martyr is essentially a witness: but a special sort of witness, one who seals his testimony with his blood. Stephen was Christ's witness and he bore his witness in three ways—by his deeds, by his words, and by his death. Hence three pictures of him emerge from the Acts of the Apostles.

1. *The deacon*

His story begins in chapter 6 with the appointment of the seven 'deacons' as they are generally called. Stephen was one of these, and the outstanding one. The task of the deacons was to relieve the apostles of their more humdrum duties and to supervise the Church's financial affairs and the distribution of alms to the poor, especially to the widows.

What sort of men were they? Surely for such a mundane job no very high qualifications were required? Evidently the apostles did not think so, for they invited the congregation to select for the business 'seven men of good report, full of the Spirit and of wisdom'. That is to say, they were to be not only men of honourable reputation and sound common-sense but also men filled with the Spirit of God. This is a point we ought not to overlook. What a difference it makes in church life when those responsible for the ordinary everyday things —treasurers, secretaries, sidesmen, choir members, cleaners— are people of spiritual calibre and deeply committed to Christ.

To return to the Church in Jerusalem: 'they chose Stephen, a man full of faith and of the Holy Spirit. . . .' A few verses further on he is described as 'full of grace and power', and the chapter ends with an account of his work in the Church. It is clear that as a deacon Stephen was not restricted to 'serving tables' and being merely an almoner, though no doubt he fulfilled his duties in a thoroughly efficient and dedicated manner. More than that, he 'did great wonders and signs among the people'; and when certain Greek-speaking Jews disputed with him about the claims of Jesus Christ, he answered their challenge in such a manner that 'they could not withstand the wisdom and the Spirit with which he spoke'.

So we come to our second picture of Stephen.

2. *The apologist*

Chapter 7 of Acts contains Stephen's *apologia* or defence when he was brought before the supreme Jewish Council in Jerusalem. The charges brought against him were that he had spoken against Moses, the law, and the temple. These probably arose from the fact that Stephen claimed that *Moses* had been superseded by Christ, the *law* by the gospel, and the *temple* by the Church.

The deacon now becomes the defender of the faith. His speech to the Council is reported at considerable length, and we cannot attempt to follow his arguments in any detail. This much however we can say. Drawing freely on the Jewish scriptures—common ground between himself and his opponents—Stephen boldly accused the Jews of being a perverse and rebellious people. They had constantly rejected the leaders God had sent them in the course of their long history. In particular he cites the case of Moses, the greatest leader of them all. The prophets had received the same sort of treatment. Hence in their attitude to Jesus the Messiah they had been acting true to type. 'You stiff-necked people, uncircumcised in heart and mind', he concluded, 'you always resist the Holy Spirit. As your fathers did, so do you.'

Stephen's *apologia* deserves the most careful study. It is a masterly piece of biblical reasoning and by it he shows himself to have been a man of brilliant intellect, dauntless courage, and gigantic spiritual stature. Surely Dr Alexander Whyte was right when he remarked, 'In the stoning of Stephen there was lost to the pentecostal church another Apostle Paul. Stephen was a young man of such original genius and of such special grace, that there was nothing he might not have attained to had he been allowed to live.'

3. *The martyr*

His opponents had no answer to Stephen's arguments—at least, not in words. So they answered him in deeds, by brute force. Hounding him out of the city they stoned him to death. But it was a glorious death for this first of martyr-saints. By the manner in which he died he bore a magnificent witness for Christ and so was a true *martus*. The deeply moving account of it all is found in the closing verses of Acts 7 (see verses 55–60).

Stephen met his end triumphantly, with the vision of the exalted Christ before his eyes; and, like his Lord, he died interceding for his murderers and with a trustful prayer of commendation on his lips. His name in the Greek, *Stephanos*, means a garland, a wreath—the victor's crown. Could any name have been more appropriate for Christ's witness? 'Be faithful unto death, and I will give you the crown of life.'

THE INNOCENTS

The world Christ knew

> Matthew 2.16 '*Herod, when he saw that he had been tricked by the wise men, was in a furious rage, and he sent and killed all the male children in Bethlehem and in all that region who were two years old or under.*

The story of the Innocents stands in stark contrast to the story of Christmas which it follows so closely. The Christmas story is all gladness. The angel proclaims 'good news', the heavenly choir breaks forth into song, the shepherds praise and glorify God, the wise men rejoice exceedingly with great joy. Now, however, joy gives place to sorrow, singing to weeping. The massacre of the babes of Bethlehem is a grim and mournful tale. What has it to say to us today? Has it anything to teach us? Surely yes.

1. *Suffering and innocence*

For one thing, here is a point at which the story of the Christ child comes very close to our own age and to the harsh realities of modern life. The world Christ knew was not so strangely remote or different from our own as we are sometimes inclined to imagine. The suffering of the innocent—and more especially of innocent children—is not some relic of a barbarous past which proud 'man come of age' has outgrown. By no means. It confronts us today in many forms and in various areas of life. It is as much a part of our world as it was of Christ's.

This is not the place to discuss the problem of suffering in general. But we must admit that that problem is never so heart-rending a tragedy as when it is the innocent who suffer. If people choose, as some do, to bring suffering on themselves by their own deliberate act, that is their responsibility. They have no one to blame but themselves. But what of those who suffer through no fault of their own and who are the victims of circumstances over which they have no control? What are we to say then? Do we say, 'God shouldn't allow it'? Do we begin to put the blame on him? Before we do that we ought to remember another fact.

2. *Suffering and evil*

While the suffering of the innocent is all tragedy, it is not all mystery. If we ask the question, 'Why do the innocent suffer?' the answer in the vast majority of cases is that it is due to human wickedness: to man's brutality, lust, depravity, avarice, callousness, and so on. And you can't blame God for that.

The massacre of the young children of Bethlehem illustrates the point. They died as a result of one man's evil. King Herod was the perpetrator of the horrible crime and what he did was in complete accord with his known character. An utterly ruthless and insanely jealous man, Herod had recently murdered two of his own sons for fear they might usurp his throne.

The fact is—and we must face the fact—behind the great mass of suffering in the world, today as in every age, in man's inhumanity to man. It was the same in the world Christ knew. So long as there are tyrants like Herod (in his day) and Hitler (in ours) occupying positions of power, the innocent are bound to suffer. There is evil in the world because there is evil in the heart of man. Here is the root problem of human life; and the gospel goes to the root of the matter by dealing first and foremost with the fact of sin. This is why the Son of God came into the world and why he was given, even before his birth, the name Jesus (Saviour). His mission was to rescue men from the power of evil, to give them a change of heart, and to make possible a new order of society.

3. *Suffering and God*

In the life of the world—the world we know as well as the world Christ knew—the forces of good and evil exist side by side and are in ceaseless conflict. Men like Herod represent the forces of evil, and, as in the case of the Bethlehem 'innocents', those evil forces often seem to triumph. What does this mean? Is sinful man the master and does he command the entire human situation? Can he do exactly as he likes? A thousand times no! The story before us reminds us that, unlikely as it may appear at the time, God is in control of history and overrules all things for his glory. The infants of Bethlehem glorified God by their deaths (see collect).

The fact is, Herod reckoned without God. His design in ordering the destruction of the children was to slay the new-born King; but his design was frustrated. By divine intervention Mary and Joseph escaped with their child to Egypt (see verses 13–15) and 'remained there until the death of Herod'. Yes, the Herods of this world do die, all of them, even the most powerful. But God *lives*—and God *reigns*! Is this why the difficult passage from the Apocalypse chosen for today's epistle depicts a vision of the heavenly throne?

What matters in the final issue is not the throne of Herod but the throne of God. The Lord reigns. The ultimate victory is with him, not with the devil. But this we must also recognise: God works out his sovereign will in the world not by sparing the innocent but by using their sufferings for his own ends. In the same way he used the sufferings of his innocent Son on Calvary to fulfil his redeeming purpose for mankind. Salvation is achieved by sacrifice. The path to glory is spattered with blood.

CIRCUMCISION OF CHRIST

The two covenants

> Luke 2.21 '*At the end of eight days, when he was circumcised, he was called Jesus, the name given by the angel before he was conceived in the womb.*'

The birth of a boy was always regarded by the Jews as a special gift from God. A son meant much more to them than a daughter and his birth was celebrated with music, dancing and song. A week after his birth, in accordance with the Jewish law, he was circumcised and at the same time he was given his name. Both ceremonies, the circumcising and the naming of the infant Jesus, are referred to in the text I have read to you and both possess a deep significance for us.

The Christian feast which celebrates this twofold event and which falls on January 1st, the eighth day after Christmas, is called in the Book of Common Prayer 'The Circumcision of Christ'. In the collect and epistle attention is focused entirely on the circumcising of the holy child and no particular reference is made to the name given to him. Yet if you look carefully at what St Luke says you will see that he refers only casually and incidentally to the act of circumcision and emphasises rather the *name* given to the child. Why? Because to us as Christians it is the name of Jesus that really matters, and all that that name implies, and not the Jewish rite of circumcision. For this reason it has been proposed that the feast we celebrate today should be changed from 'The Circumcision of Christ' to 'The Naming of Jesus'.

What are we to say to this? I would suggest that *both* the circumcision and the naming are relevant and that both deserve our attention. The one (the circumcision) looks back to the past; the other (the name of Jesus) looks forward to the future. The one links him with the old covenant of the law, the other with the new covenant of the gospel. In a word, Jesus is the link between the two covenants.

1. *The covenant of the law*

Among the Jews circumcision was far more than a physical operation, the cutting off of the foreskin. It was a distinctly religious rite, an act of initiation. Circumcision, going right back to the time of Abraham, was the 'sign of the covenant' which God made with his people Israel. So the Jewish law insisted that every male child must be circumcised on the eighth day, even if that day happened to be the sabbath. Those who were uncircumcised were said to be 'cut off' from Israel and outside the covenant.

The infant Jesus was therefore circumcised at the end of eight days and in this way, as the collect puts it, he became 'obedient to the law for man'. But clearly the ceremony had a deeper meaning than that. Circumcision was a 'sign' to the people of Israel. It was, in St Paul's words, God's *seal* upon his covenant with them, a seal of his gracious work in choosing them for his own. And one other thing. Circumcision involved the shedding of blood. Now among the Jews blood represented *life*, and the shedding of blood was the symbolic laying down of life. It may be that the blood shed in circumcision was a kind of ratification of the covenant. At any rate, as Dr Oesterley remarks, it is difficult to get away from the conviction that when a child was circumcised he was consecrated to God by virtue of the fact that his life, under the symbol of blood, was offered to the Lord.

How does this apply to the circumcision of the Christ child? Surely we are on safe ground if we say that by his circumcision he was not only made obedient to the law but was enrolled among the people of Israel, sealed with the sign of the covenant, and consecrated to the service of God. Some would go further and suggest that in his circumcision we can also see a sort of parable of the cross, a foreshadowing of the blood he was to shed in due course for man's redemption—the blood of the new covenant.

2. *The covenant of the gospel*

We are now ready to turn to the other aspect of the matter, the naming of Jesus. St Paul reminds us that when in the fullness of time God sent forth his Son, he was 'born of a woman, born under the law, to redeem those who were under the law, so that we might receive adoption as sons'. This makes clear that while Jesus belonged initially to the old covenant, he came into the world to inaugurate a new covenant. His mission was to 'redeem' or rescue men from the guilt and power of sin and to bring them into a new and vital relationship with God as his children.

That saving mission was expressed in the name given to him at his circumcision. 'He was called Jesus.' In a sense the name was quite an ordinary one. It was common enough among the Jews in those days, being the equivalent of the Hebrew name Joshua. But as applied to the child of Mary the name Jesus has a quite special significance, for it means 'saviour' or God's salvation. So the angel said to Joseph before his birth, 'You shall call his name Jesus, for he will save his people from their sins'.

Jesus is the Saviour of men. He is more than that, of course. He is also the Son of God, the Teacher, the Judge. He is the anointed Prophet, Priest and King. But the name given to him by God indicates none of these offices. Why? In order to make clear, in some very well-known words, that 'Christ Jesus came into the world to save sinners'.

Jesus is the name of our salvation. And there is salvation in no one else, for there is no other name under heaven given among men by which we must be saved (Acts 4.12). Let us take that name with us into this new year and seek to realise more fully all that it can mean to us.

> Jesus! the name that charms our fears,
> That bids our sorrows cease;
> 'Tis music in the sinner's ears,
> 'Tis life and health and peace.
>
> (C. Wesley)

CONVERSION OF ST PAUL

What is conversion?

Acts 9.5 '*"Tell me, Lord," he said, "who you are." The voice answered, "I am Jesus."*'

It strikes me as a significant fact that when the Church honours the great apostle St Paul it commemorates not his birth, nor his life, nor his missionary labours, nor his martyrdom. It commemorates his conversion. Why is this? Because the conversion of Saul of Tarsus was a decisive turning-point not only in the story of the Christian Church but in the history of mankind. It was an epoch-making event, the importance of which can hardly be over-estimated. As if to recognise that fact, St Luke relates the conversion story no less than three times in the Acts: here in chapter 9 and later in chapters 22 and 26.

We don't seem to hear much about conversion nowadays. Is it because we are inclined to fight shy of the word as being a bit old-fashioned? Is it because conversions themselves are somewhat rare events? Or is it because the Church has lost sight of its mission and is not sure whether it ought to be converting anybody? Whatever be the answer, here at any rate is a subject well worth thinking around and doubtless we can learn a good deal about it from the conversion of St Paul.

1. *Not turning religious*

There are always misunderstandings to be got out of the way in dealing with a matter like this. One of these is the notion that to be converted is to turn religious. People are inclined to think that when a man is converted to Christ he necessarily abandons a godless life and becomes pious: goes to church, says his prayers, reads the Bible, and so on.

Now, whatever happened to Saul on the Damascus road it was nothing at all like that. When he became a Christian he was already a deeply and devoutly religious man. He had been brought up in the strictest rule of the Jewish faith. He was a Pharisee. He had been trained as a rabbi. He knew his Bible thoroughly well, he prayed and fasted regularly, he carried out all the requirements of the Jewish law. In fact one might say that there was no more genuinely religious man in his day than Saul of Tarsus. You can read his own testimony to that in the third chapter of Philippians.

Clearly then for Saul 'conversion' did *not* mean turning religious or merely exchanging one religion for another. In that case what did it mean? Let us now be positive and face that question.

2. *Encounter with Christ*

One thing stands out crystal clear in each of the accounts in the Acts. In his conversion Saul of Tarsus had, as it were, a head-on collision with Jesus Christ.

Here was this man 'breathing murderous threats against the disciples of the Lord', determined to stamp out this new-fangled sect of the Nazarenes and journeying to far-off Damascus to extend his fanatical crusade of persecution. Then as he neared the city the amazing thing happened. A light from heaven flashed around him and he fell to the ground, blinded and bewildered. A voice spoke to his heart and conscience:

'Saul, Saul, why do you persecute me?'
He answered, 'Tell me, Lord, who you are.'
The voice replied, 'I am Jesus, whom you are persecuting....'

We need pursue the story no further, for here is the point of crisis. '*I am Jesus*', said the voice. It was he and no other. For Saul, conversion meant a personal encounter with the living Lord Jesus; and so amazing, so overpowering was it that he at once capitulated, laid down his arms, surrendered his soul. The fiery rebel became the willing servant. 'Lord', what do *you* want me to do?'

This personal encounter with Christ, involving total commitment to him as Saviour and Lord, is the one element common in all genuine conversions. The actual manner in which the encounter takes place varies enormously with different people and is not important. What is important is that the encounter takes place. The point I am making now is that conversion is not simply *any* kind of deep, mystical experience of the divine. It is an experience of Christ. It has no meaning apart from him.

Again, I think we ought to recognize that in the end conversion is not so much a matter of our seeking Christ, finding Christ, accepting Christ—which is the way we are inclined to talk, as though the initiative were on our side. It is in reality Christ seeking us, finding us, accepting us. The initiative lies with him. Paul came to see this most clearly as he later reflected on his own experience. When in his letters he refers to his conversion he does so in terms of what the Lord had done for him. 'It pleased God to reveal his Son in me', he wrote to the Galatians. 'Christ appeared to me', he testified to the Corinthians. 'Christ took hold of me', he told the Philippians. This is how he understood what had happened to him. He knew himself to be from first to last a debtor to God's grace.

3. *The test of conversion*

Conversion meant something tremendous for Paul. What does it mean for us? We might as well be honest and admit that we ourselves have not undergone the sort of dramatic experience that he passed through. Most of us, in all probability, can point to no day or hour or place when we first consciously encountered the Son of God and became Christians. We have no exciting story to tell, no glowing testimony to give.

Does that mean we are not converted? Mercifully it does not. As far as we are concerned there are two things that matter. The *first* is that we have come to know Christ for ourselves as the Saviour who died for us and have yielded to him as our living Lord. Nothing can take the place of this first-hand experience. A second-hand religion is simply not good enough.

The *second* thing that matters is that, quite apart from the conversion experience, we know the reality of the converted life and are living in fellowship with Christ and his people. Here is the ultimate test. Conversion is not only a change of heart. It is also a change of direction. Canon Bryan Green in his book on evangelism puts it like this: to the question, 'Is your face or your back towards Christ?' the converted man can confidently answer, 'My face'. He knows where he is going in his spiritual pilgrimage. His conversion is a beginning, not the end. He is on the King's highway and, as he journeys on day by day in the path of holiness, he can say with St Paul, 'I have not yet reached perfection, but I press on, hoping to take hold of that for which Christ once took hold of me' (Philippians 3.12, NEB).

PRESENTATION OF CHRIST

Presented with clean hearts

Luke 2.22–24 '*When the time came for their purification according to the law of Moses, they brought him up to Jerusalem to present him to the Lord (as it is written in the law of the Lord, "Every male that opens the womb shall be called holy to the Lord") and to offer a sacrifice according to what is said in the law of the Lord, "a pair of turtledoves, or two young pigeons."'*

The feast which falls today, February 2nd—the fortieth day after Christmas—has three names. It should rightly be termed 'The Presentation of Christ in the Temple', for this is the most important element in the commemoration. But as the Prayer Book says, the feast is 'commonly called The Purification of St Mary the Virgin' and this medieval title still persists. In the Middle Ages it was also known as Candlemas because of the lighted candles carried in procession to express the truth proclaimed in the *Nunc Dimittis* (part of today's gospel), that Christ had come to be 'a light to lighten the Gentiles' as well as to be the glory of his own people Israel.

Now let's turn to the verses I have read to you and find out what happened in the temple at Jerusalem that fortieth day after the birth of Jesus, and why it happened.

1. *The Jewish background*

The key to it all is to be found in the Old Testament scriptures. It is significant that no less than three times in these verses Luke tells us that the observances were carried out *according to the law* (verses 22, 23, 24)—that is, the mosaic law.

The next thing to get clear is that *two* distinct ceremonies were involved that day, the one connected with the child and the other with his mother. The first was the redemption of the firstborn son by payment of a sum of money. We read about this in Exodus 13:

'The Lord said to Moses, "Consecrate to me all the first-born; whatever is the first to open the womb among the people of Israel, both of man and of beast, is mine."'

'Every first-born of man among your sons you shall redeem.'

What was the redemption price? The answer is found in Numbers 18.16: 'Their redemption price (at a month old you shall redeem them) you shall fix at five shekels in silver, according to the shekel of the sanctuary.'

The idea behind all this was that every firstborn male child was considered to be 'holy', belonging to the Lord, in view of the sparing of Israel's firstborn on the night of the Passover; and he had therefore to be purchased back by his parents and then 'presented' to the Lord.

The other ceremony, which took place at the same time, was the purification of the mother. The law here is explained in Leviticus 12. A Jewish woman was regarded as ceremonially 'unclean' for forty days after the birth of a son and at the end of that time she was required to offer two sacrifices for her purification: a lamb for a burnt offering and a pigeon for a sin offering. Those who could not afford a lamb were allowed to offer two pigeons. This is what the mother of Jesus did. It was the poor person's offering. Only after these sacrifices had been made could the woman again take her place in society and engage in public worship.

Luke's account makes clear that both these ceremonies, the presentation of the child and the purification of the mother, were duly carried out as the law required.

2. *The Christian interpretation*

So much for the Bible story and its explanation. How are we to interpret it for ourselves? Here are three simple suggestions.

First, let us go to the New Testament and listen to what St Paul has to say in Ephesians 5:

'Christ loved the church and gave himself for her, that he might sanctify her, having cleansed her by the washing of water with the word, that the church might be presented before him in splendour, without spot or wrinkle or any such thing, that she might be holy and without blemish' (verses 25–27).

The interesting thing in this passage is that the two main ideas of the gospel narrative are combined. The Church, as the bride of Christ, is to be *presented* to the Lord in splendour and at the same time she is to be *purified* by water and the Word in order to be holy and without blemish.

Second, let us turn to the Prayer Book and make our own

beautiful collect (of eighth-century origin) appointed for this feast day. It is a prayer that we may be presented to God 'with pure and clean hearts' by his Son Jesus Christ our Lord; and once again the thought of purification is happily combined with that of presentation.

Third, let us look at the hymn-book and consult Keble's hymn for this feast, 'Blest are the pure in heart'. In actual fact only the first and third verses are Keble's, these being the opening and closing verses of his long poem for the day in his *Christian Year*. The Reverend W. J. Hall, a minor canon of St Paul's well over a century ago, took those two verses and added two of his own (verses 2 and 4) and as a result we have one of the most perfect hymns in the English language.

Blest are the pure in heart,
For they shall see our God,
The secret of the Lord is theirs,
Their soul is Christ's abode.

Still to the lowly soul
He doth himself impart,
And for his dwelling and his throne
Chooseth the pure in heart.

THE ANNUNCIATION

Mary's Magnificat

Luke 1.46 '*And Mary said:*
"*Tell out, my soul, the greatness of the Lord,*
rejoice, rejoice, my spirit, in God my saviour".'

There are occasions in life which are so overwhelming and shattering that at the time words more or less fail us and we can find little to say.

It was something like that with Mary of Nazareth when

the angel Gabriel appeared to her and announced the staggering news that God had chosen her, of all the women in the world, to be the mother of the promised Messiah. Luke's moving account in today's gospel makes it clear that at first Mary could scarcely take it in and she was reduced to bewildered silence. As the angel unfolded his message she could only protest that she had no husband, so how could she bear a son? Then the revelation was given to her: it was by the power of the Holy Spirit she was to conceive and bear a child to be called the Son of the Highest. Such was God's purpose for her. Was she willing to accept her destiny? Her consent was awaited.

Now she *must* speak; but there is no need for many words. She does not argue but in simple faith bows to the will of God. 'Here I am, at the Lord's service! As you have spoken, so let it be.'

That was all for the present. Not wordy speech but quiet submission was Mary's immediate response. But later, as you will recall, her heart overflowed in adoring praise and she voiced her thoughts in that wonderful hymn we have come to know as the *Magnificat*. Let us glance at it for a few minutes, for the familiar words enable us to see deeply into the mind of this holy and humble young woman and to understand something of the faith in which she accepted her high calling.

What is her song all about?

1. *She magnifies the grace of God*

To begin with, Mary magnifies God's mercy to herself. In the opening stanzas the praise takes on a personal note.

> Tell out, my soul, the greatness of the Lord,
> rejoice, rejoice, my spirit, in God my saviour;
> so tenderly has he looked upon his servant,
>   humble as she is.
> For, from this day forth,
> all generations will count me blessed,
> so wonderfully has he dealt with me,
>   the Lord, the Mighty One (verses 46–49, NEB).

It is noteworthy that Mary is concerned to magnify the Lord—not herself. In this she is wiser than those who in the later history of the Church have sought to exalt her rather than her Lord and have looked to her as a repository of grace. Such ideas are foreign to her. She knows herself to be but the recipient of grace. She is conscious of her own humble station as the handmaid of the Lord. She is content to see herself as his chosen instrument for the carrying out of his age-old purpose for the redemption of mankind. So she glorifies the Lord for his tender mercy and rejoices in him as her Saviour.

The Mighty One, she said, had 'dealt wonderfully' with her. Mark those words before we leave them. They are the only reference in the hymn, veiled and delicate, to the mystery of the Life already conceived in her womb. And yet the whole hymn is inspired by that mystery, and it is because of that mystery that 'all generations' have indeed counted her blessed.

2. *She celebrates the kingdom of God*

The next part of the hymn (verses 50–53) takes a wider sweep. From thinking of what the Lord has done for her the singer considers the revolutionary things he is going to accomplish in the world through the coming of the Messiah and his kingdom. These verses are prophetic of the gospel. Though expressed in the past tense they celebrate what God purposes to do in the future. They are a poetical description of the new order of society Christ is to establish: a society in which the proud will be humiliated and the mighty overthrown, the lowly will be lifted up and the hungry satisfied.

This central section of the hymn is, as Bishop John Moorman says, 'a forecast of the kingdom of God on earth, a vision of a society under the perfect control of God and in which God reigns and rules'. So Mary sings, in the words of Timothy Dudley-Smith's fine paraphrase:

> Tell out, my soul, the greatness of his might:
>   Powers and dominions lay their glory by;
> Proud hearts and stubborn wills are put to flight,
>   The hungry fed, the humble lifted high.

3. *She attests the faithfulness of God*

In the last strains of her hymn of praise Mary is mindful of God's faithfulness to 'his servant Israel' in fulfilment of his word. She recalls his first promise to his chosen people, given to 'Abraham and his seed' some 2,000 years before:

> He has helped his servant Israel,
> in remembrance of his mercy,
> as he spoke to our fathers,
> to Abraham and to his posterity for ever
> (verses 54, 55).

Mary doubtless thought of Abraham's 'seed' in terms of her own Jewish people, the descendants of Abraham after the flesh. Indeed the whole of the Magnificat has a strongly Hebrew flavour and is essentially a Messianic hymn. Much of it echoes the song of Hannah in the Old Testament (1 Samuel 2.1–10), though it rises to loftier spiritual heights.

Be that as it may, we as Christians can hardly fail to see a wider meaning in these closing words of the hymn. To us, as to St Paul, Abraham's 'seed' or offspring has a new significance: 'If you are Christ's, then *you* are Abraham's offspring, heirs according to promise.' The Church of Christ, embracing Jew and Gentile alike, is now the Israel of God. His ancient promise has received a fulfilment which Mary could not have foreseen. All the same, as we like her magnify the Lord for his mercy, we too must attest his faithfulness to his promises, and we too can sing:

> Tell out, my soul, the glories of his word:
> Firm is his promise, and his mercy sure.
> Tell out, my soul, the greatness of the Lord
> To children's children and for evermore.

ST MARK

A failure who made good

2 Timothy 4.11 *'Get Mark and bring him with you; for he is very useful in serving me.'*

'He's very useful'—such was Paul's final verdict on Mark in this his last letter. It was a fine tribute—and in some respects an unexpected one. For Paul had not always cherished such a good opinion of Mark. At one time he had been badly let down by this man and had written him off as a failure. 'He's useless in the Lord's service!' he would probably have said then if asked for his views.

Now however, at the end of his life, the apostle bears a different testimony. Mark had magnificently risen above his early failure and Paul had come to appreciate his worth. He's a useful man', he writes to Timothy. 'Get hold of him and bring him with you.'

You will rightly sense that here is a character well worth looking at, in as far as we can piece together his story from the New Testament. The story revolves around certain places, beginning in Jerusalem and ending in Rome.

1. *Jerusalem*

The first place with which Mark is associated is Jerusalem. His home was there. We may be fairly certain that he was born in the city and spent his early life in it. He had a Jewish name *John* ('The Lord is gracious') as well as *Marcus*, which was the Roman name he adopted later when he moved into the wider world outside Palestine. His mother was Mary of Jerusalem, who is mentioned in Acts 12. Nothing is said about his father, who had presumably died some time before.

The Acts reference tells us that the Jerusalem church met for prayer in the home of Mary, and this suggests that her house was a large one and that she was a woman of some means. We are probably not wrong if we think of John Mark at that time as a young, prosperous man-about-town who had lived a fairly easy sort of life. He had not as yet had to face the harsher realities of the world. I suspect that there was a certain 'softness' about his character at this stage. If so, we can better understand what happened to him a bit later on when his faith was tested.

2. *Antioch*

The next time we meet with Mark is in connection with St Paul's first missionary journey (Acts 13, 14). It started from Antioch in Syria, which at an early date became the main centre of Gentile missionary enterprise. With the blessing of the local church, Paul and Barnabas set off on their travels—'and they had John to assist them'. John Mark, it seems, went as their attendent to look after the practical details of the expedition.

At first all went well. They crossed the sea to Cyprus and here the work met with good success as they crossed the island preaching the Word of God. A notable convert was won in the person of the proconsul Sergius Paulus (the Roman governor), and doubtless many others also believed.

John Mark, we may surmise, was enjoying himself at this stage. He decided he liked being a missionary! It was very pleasant travelling around with the two illustrious apostles, especially in such a delightful spot as Cyprus. The scenery was magnificent, the climate perfect, and the Lord was blessing the work. In fact everything in the garden was lovely.

3. *Pamphylia*

The apostles left the island and set sail for the south coast of Asia Minor, arriving in due course at Perga in the province of Pamphylia. Here things were not so good, for the climate was bad in this low-lying territory.

But worse was to follow. The missionaries decided to penetrate inland across the wild and rugged Taurus mountains into the province of Galatia. An arduous journey lay ahead. All sorts of unknown difficulties and dangers might be encountered. And in all probability Paul was already a sick man.

The prospect was not an enticing one—and Mark's courage failed him. He thought longingly of his comfortable home and the friends he had left behind and he decided he was not cut out for a missionary life after all. He deserted the party, turned back, and made off post-haste for Jerusalem.

When it came to the test, Mark failed, and failed miserably. Small wonder Paul was bitterly disappointed with him. Useless! That's what he thought of John Mark. And when he and Barnabas planned their next expedition he resolutely refused to consider Barnabas's suggestion that they should take Mark with them again. The risk was too big. As the Acts story puts it, 'Paul judged that the man who deserted them in Pamphylia and had not gone on to share in their work was not the man to take with them now' (15.38, NEB).

In the end the two friends parted company on this issue. Paul chose Silas as his companion and went his way while Barnabas took Mark and set off on another journey. It was a generous gesture on the part of Barnabas to give Mark a second chance, typical of this 'son of encouragement'. And perhaps it was due to the encouragement Barnabas gave him that Mark was able to recover from his previous failure and vindicate himself. Apart from Barnabas we might never have heard of Mark again. He might have been lost to the service of Christ and his Church for the rest of his days.

4. *Rome*

We hear nothing more of Mark until the time of Paul's first imprisonment in Rome. In his letter to the Colossian Christians he sends greetings from Mark and commends him to their hospitality (4.10)—the inference being that Mark was then with the apostle in Rome. Obviously by this time—some fourteen years or so after the Pamphylian episode—Mark had established himself as a Christian man whose faith and courage none could doubt. And Paul fully trusted him.

A few years later Paul is again a prisoner in Rome, bravely awaiting the end, and as he gives Timothy his final instructions he writes the words with which we began our study: 'Get

Mark and bring him with you; for he is very useful in serving me.' Whether Mark got to Paul before he died we do not know. But a well-attested tradition asserts that Mark *was* in Rome with the apostle Peter about the same time and that it was in Rome that he wrote the gospel which bears his name, based on the preaching of Peter.

A failure? Useless? Such Mark had appeared to be at first. But by the grace of God he made good and became a fearless and useful witness for Christ. His story gives us all hope. It is full of encouragement. It enables us to say:

> Rejoice not over me, O my enemy;
> when I fall, I shall rise;
> when I sit in darkness,
> the Lord will be a light to me (Micah 7.8).

ST BARNABAS

A good man

Acts 11.24 '*He was a good man, full of the Holy Spirit and of faith.*'

When I was a student at Bristol I once heard Bishop Taylor Smith say in a sermon that no arithmetic has ever been invented that can estimate the worth of a good man. That was a great many years ago now, but the words have stuck in my mind ever since. If I remember aright the bishop was preaching about John the Baptist, but he might equally well have been dealing with another Bible character—Barnabas. For Barnabas, we are told, 'was a good man, full of the Holy Spirit and of faith'.

1. *The worth of goodness*

We are not given a great deal of information about him in the New Testament. To some extent he gets overshadowed by

St Paul. But sufficient emerges from the references to him in Acts to kindle our interest and to convince us that he was a singularly attractive apostolic man.

It seems that he was one of the early Jewish converts to the Christian faith in Jerusalem, a Levite, a native of Cyprus, and we are told that his original name was Joseph. It was the apostles who surnamed him Barnabas, which means a son of comfort or consolation. The name is significant. It provides a clue to the character of this man. The early Church evidently found in him a special source of strength and encouragement. He was a warm-hearted man, a sympathetic friend. He gave himself freely to others. He put new heart into the struggling Christian community in Jerusalem. There was something about him that radiated joy, serenity, courage. A good man indeed—and, of course, full of the Holy Spirit.

But remember, a good man is not a perfect man, and Barnabas was not without his faults. The New Testament records make that quite clear. St Paul refers to an occasion at Antioch in Syria when Barnabas revealed a strange weakness and was carried away by some Jewish Christians who were denying the gospel by imposing a sort of spiritual apartheid on the congregation. And you will recall that other and better known occasion when Barnabas and Paul had an unfortunate difference of opinion about John Mark and in the end parted company. It's not easy to discover the rights and wrongs of the matter, but in any case it takes two to make a quarrel and doubtless there were faults on both sides.

For all that, Barnabas was a good man, and I think it is noteworthy that he stands out for what he *was* and not merely for what he did. He may not have possessed outstanding gifts or a brilliant intellect, but he was a true son of consolation. He was a great encourager of others and all who came in touch with him felt better for being in his company.

2. *Ministry of encouragement*

There is a real place in life today for a ministry of encouragement—in the Church as much as anywhere else. Many

Christians, faced with difficult situations at work or in their homes, are losing heart. And things are not made any easier by the prophets of gloom who are constantly harping on the failure of the Church and would like to make us believe that Christianity as we have known it is played out and has little hope of survival.

It is, of course, the most unmitigated nonsense, and all the more inexcusable nonsense when those who talk in this way profess and call themselves Christains. But the effect of such talk can only be to undermine confidence in the cause of Christ and to spread despondency and alarm.

What the Church sorely needs in these days is a few more sons of consolation who will uplift the hearts of God's people by sounding a note of apostolic optimism and rekindling the lamps of faith. This dismal, defeatist talk is not only stupid. It is also unrealistic. After all, God is not dead—even if some of our modern theologians seem anxious to officiate at his funeral. God lives! God reigns! The last word is not with the devil or man but with Christ the exalted Son. And his promise still stands: all the powers of hell cannot prevail against the Church which he is building.

3. *Sacrificial love*

The shining goodness of Barnabas comes out in many ways in the Acts of the Apostles. Take, for example, the first glimpse we get of him (chapter 4). It was a time when the Jerusalem church was in need of funds to relieve its poorer members, and Barnabas is singled out as one who gave a splendid lead in this matter. He was the owner of a field, probably in his native Cyprus, an island renowned for its rich and fertile soil. Quite spontaneously, without the slightest pressure or compulsion, he sold the valuable property and gave the whole of the proceeds to the apostles. It was a magnificent gesture, an act of reckless generosity which strikingly illustrates the sacrificial quality of true love and true goodness.

Again, let me remind you of the magnanimous way in which Barnabas befriended the newly converted Saul of

Tarsus at that critical moment when Saul returned to Jerusalem from Damascus. Only a short while before Saul had left Jerusalem breathing out threatenings and slaughter against the disciples of the Lord. Now he comes back as a Christian—or at least claiming to be one. Not unnaturally the church members were hesitant about accepting his claim and looked upon him with suspicion and fear. What! Saul converted? Saul baptised? Saul a servant of Christ? Surely not!

If ever Saul needed a friend it was now. And he found one. 'Barnabas took him, and brought him to the apostles, and declared to them how on the road he had seen the Lord, and how at Damascus he had preached boldy in the name of Jesus.' In doing this Barnabas showed the bigness of his heart, the warmth of his nature, the strength of his friendship. He risked his reputation for Saul. As Dr Alexander Whyte remarked, he took Saul to his heart at a time when every other heart in Jerusalem was hardened against him; and for that alone he deserves our honour and our love for ever.

He was 'a good man'. That is his abiding epitaph in scripture. It does not say he was a *great* man, though he possessed some genuinely great qualities. But he was most certainly a good man, and it is more important to be good than to be great. In actual fact it is given to few to achieve greatness. It is open to us all to be good—through being full of the Holy Spirit and of faith.

ST JOHN BAPTIST

The making of a prophet

Luke 7.26, 27 '*What did you go out to see? A prophet? Yes, I tell you, and more than a prophet. This is he of whom it is written, "Behold, I send my messenger before thy face, who shall prepare thy way before thee".*'

What Christ thinks of men is always more important than

what they think of themselves, or what others think. Why do I say that? Because in the words I have read to you we have our Lord's estimate of a man—John the Baptist. The tribute he pays him is a magnificent one. John is not only a prophet but more than a prophet. He is the Lord's messenger foretold by Malachi. Of those born of women there has arisen none greater than John (verse 28).

Is that how John thought of himself? By no means! In his own eyes he was a mere nobody, simply a voice crying in the wilderness to prepare the way of the coming King. Nor did the church leaders of the day think much of him. Failing to recognise his spiritual authority they dismissed him as a religious crank and fanatic and paid no attention to his words. And as for King Herod, representing the secular arm—Herod 'that fox', as Jesus called him—he thought so little of John that he had him arrested, imprisoned, beheaded.

But the Lord's opinion of John, as we have seen, was entirely different. He saw in his forerunner a man of true greatness, that is, of moral and spiritual greatness, a prophet of the Highest—indeed, the last and greatest of all the prophets.

This raises an important question. How did John become so great a man? After all, a man does not achieve greatness of this kind by accident, nor does it happen overnight. Can we discern some of the factors that contributed to the making of this prophet? I think we can.

1. *The hand of the Lord*

To begin with, we must recognise that there were supernatural elements in the story of John's birth. He was the child of promise, born to his parents in their old age. Some remarkable prophecies were spoken about him, both before and after his birth, marking him out as a man destined to fulfil, in the providence of God, a unique and exalted ministry. When the angel of the Lord appeared to his father Zechariah the priest, in the temple, he spoke these words concerning the child to be born:

He will be great before the Lord,
and he shall drink no wine nor strong drink,
and he will be filled with the Holy Spirit,
even from his mother's womb.
And he will turn many of the sons of Israel to the
Lord their God....

In due course God fulfilled his word. As the collect puts it, John was 'wonderfully born' to his aged parents, filled with the Spirit from birth, set apart as a Nazarite and dedicated to the prophetic office he was to fulfil after the order of Elijah. Whatever else we may have to say about the making of this man, one thing is clear. He was not a self-made man. He was made by God. There is a revealing sentence a bit later in Luke's account of him which says, 'the hand of the Lord was with him' (1.66). Here surely is the ultimate secret of all that John was and all that he became. Just as the hand of the potter moulds the clay and makes it what he wants, so the hand of the Lord fashioned the life of this man and equipped him for his prophetic role.

2. *The influence of the home*

On the human level a formative factor in the training of John was his home life. He enjoyed the immense privilege of a godly upbringing. His father Zechariah was a priest, well versed in the things of God and a man of prayer. His mother Elizabeth, a kinswoman of the Virgin Mary, possessed a devout faith and accepted the gift of her child as a solemn trust from God. We may be sure that in their simple home in the hill-country of Judaea the boy was brought up in the fear and nurture of the Lord. Day by day he would be faithfully instructed in the holy scriptures and nourished in the life of prayer. Above all, he would be taught about the 'hope of Israel', the coming of the long-promised Messiah, and of the part which John himself was to play as his herald and forerunner.

At the time of John's birth his father had prophesied:

> You, my child, shall be called the prophet of the
> Highest,
> for you will go before the Lord to prepare his ways,
> to give knowledge of salvation to his people
> in the forgiveness of their sins.

To the fulfilment of that high destiny John was prepared and trained by his parents from the very beginning. Their holy lives as well as their faithful instruction must have made a profound impression on him as he passed from boyhood to youth. No wonder Luke remarks, 'The child grew and became strong in spirit'. That is, physical growth was matched by increasing spiritual strength. Then Luke adds: 'he was in the wilderness till the day of his manifestation to Israel.' That brings us to the third factor in the making of the prophet.

3. *The school of the desert*

The time came (perhaps it was after the death of his parents) when John left his home in the hills and went off into the lonely wilderness around the Dead Sea. The time to begin his public ministry had not yet arrived. He must be further equipped for the task that awaited him. The desert was his final training school.

What was John doing in the desert? He was not having a holiday or enjoying a rest-cure. I would rather suggest that for a while he was getting away from the haunts of men in order to be alone with God. He was deliberately abandoning the world, with all its haste and clamour and distractions, so that in the silence and solitude of the wilderness he might be able to listen to the voice of the Spirit and learn the will of God.

This is not a popular idea nowadays. According to the modern pundits, the Church must not withdraw from the world or be different from the world but must totally identify itself with the world and fully share the life of the world. 'Worldly holiness'—that's the current phrase. Of course there is truth in this concept, and I would be the first to admit it. But the stories of the Church's saints and heroes remind us that it is not the whole truth. Would John have been the great man he was if he had not spent time in the desert, deepening his communion with God? During those hidden years the desert was not only his physical environment. It was also his training college, his theological seminary, his school of prayer. Here I believe is a vital clue to this man's character and life and work.

But note: 'he was in the wilderness *until the day of his manifestation to Israel.*' John did not stay in the desert. When God's hour struck he emerged from it, and the voice of prophecy, which had been silent for centuries, rang out again in Israel, announcing the advent of God's kingdom and calling the nation to repentance. And the ordinary people, recognising the authentic word of the Lord, flocked to hear him and be baptised. That is why later on, when Jesus talked to the crowds about John, he asked, 'What was the spectacle that drew you to the wilderness? A reed-bed swept by the wind? No? Then what did you go out to see? A man dressed in silks and satins? Surely you must look in palaces for grand clothes and luxury. But what did you go out to see? A prophet? Yes indeed, and far more than a prophet. He is the man of whom Scripture says,

> "Here is my herald, whom I send on ahead of you,
> and he will prepare your way before you." '

ST PETER

Man of rock

> Matthew 16.18 ' "*You are Peter, and on this rock I will build my church*".'

It was Jesus who gave Simon his new name. When Andrew his brother introduced him to the Lord, we are told that the Lord looked him in the face and said, 'You are Simon, son of

John. You shall be called Cephas.' *Cephas* is an Aramaic word meaning 'rock'. *Petros* is its Greek equivalent, and so we get our English name Peter.

Man of rock—that's what Jesus called Simon. Why? Because he was then that sort of man? No. At the time, as the gospel stories show, Simon was unstable, impetuous, inconsistent. There was an element of weakness in his makeup. But when Jesus looked at him that day and gave him his new name he saw not the man Simon *was* but the man he would become. Jesus himself was going to make of him a strong, resolute, steadfast character—a man of rock.

It is against this background that we must consider the passage that forms today's gospel and the words which I have given you for my text.

1. *Peter's confession*

'Who do men say that the Son of Man is?' This was the first of two questions Jesus put to the disciples when he took them apart in the region of Caesarea Philippi. It was a general question and they answered it in general terms. The second question was more personal. 'But you', he asked, 'who do *you* say that I am?' Simon Peter answered, 'You are the Messiah, the Son of the living God.'

It was a tremendous affirmation of faith. And it earned for Peter a special benediction: 'Blessed are you, Simon Bar-Jona! For flesh and blood has not revealed this to you, but my Father in heaven. And I tell you, you are Peter (*Petros*) and on this rock I will build my church, and the powers of Hades shall never prevail against it.'

One thing is made perfectly clear. Peter's apprehension of Jesus as the Messiah was not a human discovery. It was a divine disclosure. His confession of faith was therefore based on revelation, not on speculation.

2. *The rock*

But what did Jesus mean when he said '*on this rock* I will build my church'? Was he not referring to Peter and using his name in a word play? Obviously so. And yet at first sight this seems rather odd. Are we to conclude that after all the Church of Christ is built on *man*? If so, then why do we sing that the Church's one foundation is Jesus Christ her Lord? And why did St Paul write, 'No other foundation can anyone lay than that which is laid, which is Jesus Christ'?

The answer is quite simple, provided two things are kept in mind. The first is that in making use of this particular analogy and likening the Church to a building, the Lord is speaking of himself not in terms of the foundation but in a different capacity—and a more important one. He is the Church's *builder*. 'I will build my Church,' he declares.

What then of the foundation? Here is the second thing to remember. It was not to the 'flesh and blood' Peter that Jesus spoke these words—not to Peter as an ordinary human being. It was to Peter as an apostolic man: a man in possession of the heavenly secret, a man who had grasped the truth about the person of Jesus, a man who had confessed Jesus to be the promised Messiah, the Son of the living God.

It was to this Peter that the Lord addressed his words. He meant: 'On this kind of rock—on Peter and others like him who possess and confess the truth about me—I will build my Church in the world.'

3. *The Church of Christ*

It is a simple fact of history that all down the centuries Christ has been building his Church on this sort of rock—'upon the foundation of the apostles and prophets', in St Paul's words (Ephesians 2.20). The Church would not exist in the world at all were it not for the faith and labours of apostolic men like Peter who, having received the truth from God, hold it fast, boldly proclaim it, live it out, and, if need be, die for it, as Peter himself did at the last.

Trace the story of the Church in any land, or in any particular locality, and you will find the record studded with the names of people of this kind who were its foundation stones.

But let's be perfectly sure that the Church is not a human

product. Christ is its builder—not Peter or any other man. Men may construct a religious institution. Only Christ can build his Church. And he is building it still in the world of our day. All he needs to carry on his building operations is dedicated men and women filled with his Spirit who acknowledge him to be the Lord and who humbly place their lives at his disposal.

One other thing. Just as Christ is the builder of the Church, so is he its *owner*. He calls it '*my* Church'. In the end this is the most important thing about the Church. It belongs to Christ. It's not Peter's church, or yours and mine. It doesn't belong to us but to him. 'Christ loved the Church and gave himself up for her'. For

> From heaven he came and sought her
> To be his holy bride,
> With his own blood he bought her,
> And for her life he died.

The Church is Christ's. This means that if we belong to the Church we belong to him. Let us never forget that. And let us give him back the life we owe, that we may play our part in the building of his Church in the world of today.

ST MARY MAGDALENE

Grace abounding

> Mark 16.9 '*When he (Jesus) rose early on the first day of the week, he appeared first to Mary Magdalene, from whom he had cast out seven demons.*'

When John Bunyan, towards the end of his twelve years' imprisonment in Bedford jail, wrote his spiritual autobiography he gave it the title of *Grace Abounding to the Chief of Sinners*. This was because, like St Paul, Bunyan could never forget the sort of man he had been and what the saving grace of Christ had done for him. So he recalled the apostle's words to Timothy, 'Christ Jesus came into the world to save sinners; of whom I am chief. Howbeit for this cause I obtained mercy, that in me first Jesus Christ might show forth all long-suffering. . . .'

Mary Magdalene, of whom we are thinking today, could have echoed that testimony. She too had been a great sinner. She too had found a great Saviour.

What does the New Testament tell us about her?

1. *The old life*

The facts are simply stated. And first as regards her name. Mary Magdalene simply means Mary of Magdala and indicates the place from which she came. Magdala was a small town on the Sea of Galilee, not far from Capernaum, with none too savoury a reputation. Twice in the gospels (Luke and Mark) she is described as one out of whom the Lord Jesus cast 'seven demons'. What are we to make of that? Opinions differ, but the figure *seven* would seem to be symbolical and to indicate that before her deliverance Mary had been completely abandoned to and possessed by evil powers.

Christian tradition has been somewhat too ready to assume that she had been a woman of immoral character. In fact, not to put too fine a point on it, that she had been a prostitute. That may have been the case, though there is really no warrant for identifying her (as is commonly done) with 'the woman of the city who was a sinner' of whom Luke tells us (chapter 7) and who washed the feet of Jesus with her penitential tears. Yet undoubtedly Mary had one thing in common with that unnamed woman. Like her, *she loved much.* And again like her, she loved much because she had been forgiven much, because the Lord had done so much for her. He had pardoned her, liberated her, transformed her, remade her. Small wonder she loved him!

How did she show her love? In service. There is a revealing passage in Luke's gospel which tells us that a small company of devoted women accompanied Jesus and the twelve in their preaching missions through Galilee and that these women 'provided for them out of their means' (8.3). Among them is mentioned 'Mary, called Magdalene, from whom seven demons had gone out'. This was her way of expressing gratitude to her Lord. She knew she had been saved to serve.

2. *Mary at the cross*

We next meet with Mary on the day of the passion. She is watching at the cross as Jesus dies. No doubt it was her love that drew her there—and kept her there. It must have caused her deep anguish of spirit to witness the sufferings of her Lord. Yet she could not leave him. Indeed, it seems she lingered there, together with one or two other women, after the other disciples had gone away. Perhaps they could stand the sight no longer. Perhaps their faith had collapsed in ruins and their hope was dead. Who could blame them?

But Mary waited there. She waited and watched till at last the sacred body was taken down from the cross. She noted carefully where it was laid to rest in Joseph of Arimathea's garden tomb. Then she and her companions returned home and prepared their burial spices.

3. *Mary at the tomb*

So the next glimpse we get of her is on the morning of the resurrection as she comes again to the grave with the ointments. She is the first to discover the empty tomb—and the first to meet with the risen Lord. 'When he rose early on the first day of the week, he appeared first to Mary Magdalene. . . .'

The story of that dramatic encounter is related in John's gospel. You recall how at first she mistook her Lord (and she still called him *Lord*, for her devotion had not died) for the gardener. But he had only to utter one word for her to recognise him. That word was 'Mary'. No one else could speak her name like that. 'Rabboni!' was her exultant reply —'My Master!' And immediately she was at his feet, clinging to him with passionate devotion. But gently he told her not to clasp him in that manner. Later on she would indeed be able to hold him fast—by faith. Meanwhile he had an urgent and joyful mission for her to fulfil, and she hastened away to the disciples with the thrilling news, 'I have seen the Lord!'

She who had been the first witness of the resurrection became the first preacher of the resurrection.

After that she disappears from the story of the New Testament. But she was doubtless among 'the women' mentioned in Acts (1.14) who with the other disciples awaited the coming of the Comforter on the day of Pentecost and who in due course were 'all filled with the Holy Spirit'. Think what that meant for Mary Magdalene. As it has been said, she who had been possessed with seven demons of evil was filled with the sevenfold Spirit of God.

ST JAMES

The first martyr-apostle

> Matthew 20.22 '*Jesus answered, "You do not know what you are asking. Are you able to drink the cup that I am to drink?"*'

In the *Te Deum* we sing,

> The glorious company of the apostles praise thee.
> The noble army of martyrs praise thee.

The man whom the Church commemorates today—James the son of Zebedee, or James the Great as he is often called—has the distinction of belonging both to that glorious company and to that noble army. For he was one of our Lord's chosen twelve and also the first of them to lay down his life for the Faith.

This would suggest that James was a man of some eminence in the story of the early Church, yet strangely enough we know next to nothing about him. In fact he has been described as the most tantalisingly vague figure among the twelve. His name always appears among the first three in all the lists of the apostles, and along with Peter and his brother John he belonged to the most intimate circle of our Lord's friends. It is strange then that so little is told us about him in the pages of the New Testament.

What can we discover about James?

1. *Son of thunder*

In the gospels he is never mentioned on his own. He always appears in the company of his brother John. Although he was the older of the two, he seems to have been overshadowed by John, in much the same way as Andrew was eclipsed by his brother Simon Peter.

James and John were the sons of Zebedee. Like their father they were Galilean fishermen. Jesus called them to become fishers of men; and, as today's collect reminds us, James, 'leaving his father and all that he had, without delay was obedient to the calling of Jesus Christ, and followed him'. Later the Lord enrolled the two brothers among his twelve apostles and gave them a nickname—*Boanerges*, 'sons of thunder' (Mark 3.17).

It's worth taking note of that name. Jesus used it to describe the character of the two brothers. They were evidently men of volcanic temperament—fiery, impetuous, liable to flare up at any moment. St Luke gives us an example of this. On the way to Jerusalem Jesus and his disciples approached a Samaritan village and asked for hospitality. The villagers refused the request; whereupon James and John exploded with indignation. 'Lord', they cried, 'shall we call down fire from heaven to burn them up?' But Jesus rebuked them and they went to another village.

On the surface the incident hardly redounds to the credit of the two brothers. It looks as though they were quick-tempered, vindictive, intolerant men. Yet their indignant outburst did at least make clear how intensely jealous they were for the honour of their Master. They were not prepared to see him insulted to his face without raising their voice in protest. Admittedly their zeal ran away with them and they spoke foolishly. All the same their zeal was genuine and they were not ashamed to show it.

Such a man was the apostle James: not a luke-warm, faint-hearted disciple but a son of thunder, a man with fire in his bones.

2. *Sharer of Christ's cup*

We turn next to the story which forms today's gospel: the request of James and John to sit on Christ's right hand and left hand in his kingdom. How did the Lord deal with them?

'Jesus turned to the brothers and said, "You do not understand what you are asking. Can you drink the cup that I am to drink?" "We can", they replied. He said to them, "You shall indeed share my cup; but to sit at my right or left is not for me to grant. . . . " ' (NEB).

Once again the brothers were rebuked, for once again they had blundered. Yet once again there is something to be said to their credit. Their request showed that they had faith in Jesus and his kingdom. They believed he was going to triumph and reign, despite all appearances to the contrary—and they wanted to be as near as possible to him in the hour of his victory. The incident shows them as examples of divine optimism and victorious faith. 'James and John never doubted that Jesus Christ was a King' (W. Barclay).

The question Jesus put to them was a searching one. 'Can you drink the cup that I am to drink?' In saying that, he was testing their devotion. They had spoken about sharing his glory. He questioned them about their capacity to share his suffering, his sacrifice, his shame. The 'cup' was plainly a reference to his coming passion; the cup which he prayed in Gethsemane might be taken from him; the cup which on the cross he took and drained to the last bitter dregs for the salvation of mankind.

'Are you able to drink of my cup?' Jesus asked. Are you willing to be rejected, to suffer and to die?

The brothers accepted the challenge. They professed themselves ready to drink of Christ's cup, and he assured them that they would indeed do so. What happened in the case of James?

3. *The martyr*

Here is the answer. 'About that time Herod the king laid violent hands upon some who belonged to the church. He killed James the brother of John with the sword.' In that glorious moment, when he died at the hands of this vain and unscrupulous monarch, James drank of the Lord's cup and (who can doubt) secured a place at his side in glory everlasting.

One question remains. Why, of all the apostles in Jerusalem, did Herod choose James the son of Zebedee to be his victim? The answer seems to me to be fairly obvious. It was because James was a particularly dangerous man as far as Herod and the Jews were concerned. The quality of his Christian life and witness made him a marked man, a man to be feared and hated by his enemies, and therefore a man to be got out of the way as soon as possible.

If this is correct, then his martyrdom throws a flood of light on James's character. He was a man whose life told for something. He could not be ignored. The 'son of thunder' had lost none of his burning faith and fervour. The flame of devotion to Christ still blazed as brightly as ever.

Such a man was James. And ourselves? What sort of Christians are we? Do our lives count for Christ? Or is our religion so nominal, our faith so feeble, our witness so innocuous, that we give the devil no particular cause for concern?

THE TRANSFIGURATION

Listen to him!

Luke 9.35 '*A voice came out of the cloud, saying, "This is my Son, my Chosen; listen to him!"*'

Probably some of you here have been to the Holy Land and visited the Sea of Galilee. If so, you will almost certainly remember the splendid view to the north of the lake, with the shining heights of Mount Hermon rising in the distance. Those mountain heights played an important part in gospel history. It was there, beyond question, that the transfiguration took place—the event we commemorate today.

We know the story well enough but perhaps we are not really clear what it means. The three chosen witnesses, the two mysterious visitors from the other world, the overshadowing cloud, the voice from heaven—and Jesus himself the centre of it all in his transfigured glory—what are we to make of it? How are we to understand it? Is there a key to the story?

1. *The key to the story*

There is a key. It is to be found I believe in the time-note with which, in every case, the story is introduced. 'After six days' the record begins in Matthew and Mark. 'About eight days after' says Luke's account. What the evangelists are saying is that the scene on Mount Hermon took place approximately a week after some other event.

What was that other event? It was the occasion when the Lord took his disciples apart into the quieter regions of the north of Palestine and at Caesarea Philippi questioned them about himself.

'Who do you say that I am?' he asked them. Immediately Simon Peter made the great confession: 'You are the Messiah, the Son of the living God!' It was a tremendous affirmation of faith. And Jesus accepted it. It was true. He was indeed the promised Messiah, the Lord's Anointed. But at once he proceeded to tell the disciples in the most solemn manner the kind of Messiah he was: a suffering Messiah. He was going to Jerusalem not to reign in glory but to die a shameful death. Such was his appointed destiny.

The disciples were horrified and scandalised. They found it impossible to accept the idea of a crucified Messiah. They refused point-blank to believe it. Such a notion seemed clean contrary to what the scriptures had foretold—and Peter felt it incumbent upon him to say so. 'God forbid, Lord! This shall never happen to you.'

Here were men perfectly prepared to believe in Jesus up to a point. But only up to a point. Beyond that point they were not willing to go. The cross was a stumbling-block to them. It is so often the same today.

2. *On the mount*

How did the Lord meet this situation? A week later he took three of those disciples, Peter, John and James, up Mount Hermon, a little to the north of Caesarea Philippi. And what happened on the mountain? Three things in particular.

In the first place, Jesus was transfigured before the disciples in dazzling brightness and they beheld him in his true glory as the Son of God.

Secondly, two of the great saints of the old covenant, Moses and Elijah, appeared in glory with him and spoke about his coming passion.

Thirdly, the voice of the Father was heard from heaven, addressing the awe-struck disciples and saying, 'This is my Son, my Chosen. Listen to him!'

Such is the story. Perhaps we are now in a position to understand its significance and to see what it is all about. The transfiguration was in fact *a revelation of the person of Christ and a vindication of his cross.*

Peter had confessed him to be the very Son of God, the glorious Messiah of prophecy. And so he was. There on the mountain top Peter and his companions caught a glimpse of his divine splendour, and their faith was confirmed and assured. They were not mistaken in their estimate of Jesus. He was indeed the Christ, the Son of the living God.

But what about the cross? That had seemed all wrong as far as they we concerned. It did not fit in with their preconceived ideas of messiahship. Yet here on the mountain were Moses and Elijah, representing the law and the prophets, not only talking with Jesus but talking about his '*exodus*' (so the Greek word is) which he was to accomplish at Jerusalem.

To Moses, at least, the exodus was a very familiar subject. He had been the leader of the exodus: that mighty deliverance which God had wrought for his people from the bondage of Egypt. At Jerusalem the Lord Jesus was to achieve a yet mightier deliverance—through his passion.

This was the theme of the conversation on the mount. Clearly enough, then, the cross was not outside the purpose of God for his beloved Son. It was in full accord with the teaching of the law and the prophets.

3. *The word of the Father*

The appearance of the two celestial visitors was obviously significant. But perhaps even more significant was their *disappearance*. A cloud overshadowed them, and when it passed Moses and Elijah had vanished. The law and the prophets had been fulfilled—and fulfilled in Jesus. So when the disciples looked up they saw no one but 'Jesus only'.

After the vision came the voice. From out of the cloud (and in scripture the cloud so often symbolises the glorious presence of God) the voice of the Father was heard, speaking to the disciples and expressing approval of his beloved Son as he set his face towards Jerusalem, there to accomplish the new and more costly 'exodus' for man's redemption.

'Listen to him!' Such was the final word of the Father to the three chosen witnesses. It was a word they sorely needed to hear. Before, when Jesus had spoken to them about the cross, they had not wanted to listen. They had scorned the subject. 'Heaven forbid!' Peter had exclaimed. They thought they knew better than their Lord. They wanted him to listen to *them*. No, said the voice on the mount. You listen to *him*.

That message is the same for us today. As St Paul put it, 'Let the word of Christ dwell in you richly'. It is in truth our highest wisdom to listen to his word, so as to bring our thoughts and ideas into harmony with his teaching. Why? Because of who he is. And the transfiguration story tells us exactly who he is. It reveals him to us as the crucified Son of Man and the glorified Son of God: as the one in whom the promises of holy scripture are fulfilled and the good pleasure of the Father is perfectly realised.

If Christ is such, what then? There is only one logical consequence. *Listen to him!*

ST BARTHOLOMEW

A dream that came true

> John 1.51 '*Jesus said to him, "Truly, truly, I say to you, you will see heaven opened, and the angels of God ascending and descending upon the Son of man."*'

Do you believe in dreams? By which I really mean, do you believe that dreams come true? You probably don't! And probably you are right. It seems generally agreed that dreams reflect the past rather than project the future; and in any case they are usually so wildly improbable as to be miles removed from reality.

Perhaps you are wondering what all this has to do with St Bartholomew and with the text I have given you. Let me explain. The words of the text were spoken by Jesus to Nathanael, and there are good grounds for believing that Nathanael and Bartholomew were one and the same person. We need not now go into the reasons for this. For the present purpose let us accept the identification, as is generally done by New Testament scholars. We may then get another point clear. When Jesus said to Nathanael (Bartholomew) that he would see the angels ascending and descending on the Son of man he was alluding to a famous Old Testament story—the story of Jacob's dream at Bethel.

1. *Jacob*

Now we are back at dreams again and we come to the real starting point in our understanding of Nathanael and the way Jesus dealt with him. The key to it all is the patriarch Jacob. It has been suggested that while Nathanael sat 'under the fig tree' (that is, in the secret place of prayer) he had been meditating on the story of Jacob and that this is the significance of the words Jesus spoke as he saw him approaching: 'Behold, an Israelite indeed, in whom is no guile!' Be careful not to miss the point. *Israel* was the new name God gave to Jacob after he had wrestled with the angel at Peniel and had become a new man. The old Jacob had been a man of guile who had won his way through life by deceit. The new Israel was a spiritual prince who had prevailed with God.

You can see then what Jesus meant when he described Nathanael as a true son of Israel. He meant that he was an utterly sincere man, a man in whom there was none of the old Jacob. And it was to this transparently honest, open-hearted man, who having sought and found the truth had made his great confession of faith, that Jesus gave the promise: 'Truly, truly, I say to you, you will see heaven opened, and the angels of God ascending and descending upon the Son of man.'

2. *The dream*

Let me remind you of Jacob's dream. At the time the patriarch was fleeing from his brother Esau whom he had defrauded and deceived. Coming to the mountainous region of Ephraim he was overtaken by nightfall, and so lay down to sleep in the open air with a stone for his pillow. And as he slept he dreamed:

'He dreamed that there was a ladder set up on the earth, and the top of it reached to heaven; and behold, the angels of God were ascending and descending on it! And behold, the Lord stood above it . . .' (Genesis 28.12, 13).

It was a remarkable dream. Jacob saw a ladder or staircase linking earth and heaven, reaching from the very place where he was right up to the throne of God—symbolising man and

God in unbroken fellowship. Moreover, on that ladder there was constant traffic as angelic messengers passed swiftly up and down on errands of mercy—symbolising earth in communication with heaven, and heaven with earth.

Then Jacob awoke from his sleep, only to discover that the whole thing was a dream. A marvellous dream indeed—but only a dream. And a dream it remained until Jesus came. And then the dream came true.

3. *The reality*

It was Jesus himself who explained to Nathanael (or Bartholomew) the meaning of the dream and how it was to find fulfilment: 'You will see heaven wide open, and God's angels ascending and descending upon the Son of Man' (NEB). There's no mistaking Jesus' words. Jacob in his dream had seen the angels ascending and descending a ladder uniting earth and heaven. The promise to Nathanael was that he and his fellow disciples would 'see' (that is, with the eye of faith) something more wonderful: the angels ascending and descending *upon the Son of Man*. And the Son of Man is Jesus himself. *He* is the ladder represented in the dream: the true ladder which has its foot on earth where *we* are in all our need, and its top in heaven where *God* is in his boundless grace and power.

What of the angels ascending and descending? Surely we cannot mistake their significance. If the ladder portrays the fact that through Christ God and man are reconciled, the angels symbolise the further truth that in him heaven and earth are in constant communication. Through him, the Mediator, all God's gifts and benedictions and mercies descend to us; and in the same way, through him our prayers and aspirations and devotions ascend to the Father and are acceptable in his sight.

The message of this dream that came true is unmistakable. Heaven opened! Paradise restored! Sinners reconciled! God accessible! Here is good news for us all on this feast of St Bartholomew. Let us make that good news our own.

ST MATTHEW

The converted tax collector

Matthew 9.9 '*As Jesus passed on from there, he saw a man named Matthew sitting at the tax office; and he said to him, "Follow me." And he rose and followed him.*'

That's an odd phrase which occurs in today's collect—'the inordinate love of riches'. What exactly does it mean? My dictionary defines *inordinate* as excessive, immoderate, passing all bounds. So when we pray for grace to forsake all covetous desires and the inordinate love of riches, we are asking that we may have a right view of money and not make it the consuming, all-absorbing passion of our life.

But another question arises. Why do we make this our prayer on the feast of St Matthew the apostle? The answer is that Matthew, before he became a disciple of Jesus, *had* an 'inordinate love of riches.' And that's the right starting-point for our study of this man.

1. *A man who loved money*

'Matthew loved money.' With those words Dr Alexander Whyte begins his chapter on the apostle in his *Bible Characters*. He goes on: 'Matthew, like Judas, must have money. With clean hands if he could; but, clean or unclean, Matthew must have money. Now, the surest way and the shortest way for Matthew to make money in the Galilee of that day was to take sides with Caesar and to become one of Caesar's tax-gatherers. This, to be sure, would be for Matthew to sell himself to the service of the oppressors of his people; but Matthew made up his mind and determined to do it.'

That gives us a sketch of the kind of man Matthew was and why he followed his chosen profession—and why, again, he would have been so heartily detested and despised by his fellow-countrymen. The tax collectors (or 'publicans' as the AV calls them, because they were men engaged in public service) were undoubtedly a pretty bad lot. No self-respecting

Jew would have anything to do with them. Not only were they written off as traitors to their own nation: they were known to be shamelessly dishonest rogues mixed up in a gigantic financial racket.

Such a man was Matthew. Money had become his idol. He worshipped mammon. He was resolved to get rich, and to get rich as quickly as possible, even if it meant robbing the poor, fleecing his own people, being ostracised by society and excommunicated by the Church. As a result, he was probably already a wealthy man, cherishing dreams of becoming wealthier still and eventually retiring to enjoy his old age in peace and comfort.

2. *A man who found true riches*

Then something changed all that. Or rather, not something but *someone*. For it was Jesus who brought about the sudden, dramatic transformation in the life of this money-grubbing tax collector. Matthew was converted. How did it happen?

The gospels paint the scene. Jesus was preaching at Capernaum where Matthew had his customs office—and Matthew heard him. Probably he had heard him many times before, and the more he listened the more clearly he saw himself as he really was and the narrow, impoverished, worthless life he was leading. At the same time he began to glimpse something of the new life Jesus was offering men under the kingly rule of God.

Maybe it happened like this. On a never-to-be-forgotten day Jesus, when he had finished preaching, stepped across to Matthew's office, paused for a moment, looked him in the face, and said quite simply, 'Follow me'. Matthew, it seems, said nothing, but he acted without hesitation. 'He rose and followed him'—that was all. But for Matthew the result was a transforming and liberating experience. Charles Wesley has described it in memorable lines:

> Long my imprisoned spirit lay,
> Fast bound in sin and nature's night;

Thine eye diffused a quickening ray,
I woke, the dungeon flamed with light;
My chains fell off, my heart was free:
I rose, went forth, and followed thee.

It was like that for Matthew. This man who had loved money was released from his 'covetous desires'. He found a new love, and the new love drove out the old. That new love was supremely the love of Jesus for him. At the same time he made another discovery: in abandoning his money-making he had suddenly become rich! He had found a new sort of riches—what St Paul calls 'the unsearchable riches of Christ'. Like St Augustine he could say, 'I gave up all for Christ, and what did I find? I found all in Christ'. Wealth was his now such as he had never dreamed of before, and his heart was filled with thankfulness and praise.

3. *A man who shared his wealth*

But it didn't all end there. The collect I have quoted reminds us that Jesus called Matthew from the receipt of custom 'to be an Apostle and Evangelist'. An apostle is a missionary; an evangelist is a gospeller. Both offices are concerned with sharing and spreading the good news about Jesus. Matthew made it his business to set about doing this from the very beginning. His first action, as Luke makes clear, was to hold a great feast for Jesus in his own house and to ask all his old companions to come along and meet Jesus. It was his way of introducing them to the Friend of sinners—and a very sensible way. I think we can learn something from Matthew about the strategy of evangelism. A lot of people will come to a party who wouldn't come to a prayer meeting.

Matthew spread the good news of Jesus in another way. We open our New Testament and are at once confronted with 'The Gospel according to Matthew'. Hence the point of the remark that when Matthew left all to follow Jesus he took his pen and ink with him. In actual fact scholars nowadays are by no means sure of the exact relation between our present gospel and the converted tax collector; but it seems likely that Matthew made a collection of the sayings of Jesus and that these sayings were incorporated into the first gospel—to form what is in fact its most prominent and valuable feature. In that case we owe Matthew an incalculable debt for preserving to us so much of our Lord's teaching.

So we leave our story: the story of a man who found in the Lord Jesus a new love, a new life, a new liberty, and who through the written gospel has been doing what he did at the first—introducing others to Jesus, the great Physician, who came to call sinners to repentance.

ST LUKE

The work of an evangelist

2 Timothy 4.11 '*Only Luke is with me.*'

It is a happy coincidence that in the passage appointed for today's epistle, in which St Paul makes this touching reference to Luke's fidelity in staying with him to the bitter end, he also gives to Timothy the solemn charge, 'Do the work of an evangelist' (verse 4). For today, as we commemorate St Luke, we think of him primarily as 'the Evangelist'. That is the title given to him in the Book of Common Prayer and the collect refers to him as 'Luke the Physician, whose praise is in the Gospel', whom God called 'to be an Evangelist and Physician of the soul'.

Let us begin by facing two questions. The first is perfectly simple and can be dealt with very quickly. What do we mean by an evangelist? The answer is that an evangelist is a person—any person—who makes known the evangel, the gospel, the good news of Jesus Christ, and communicates it to others. The second question is the practical one: how do we set about that task? In the apostle's words, what does it mean to do the work of an evangelist? This is a more difficult question and calls for a more detailed answer.

In general terms, and the answer is very general, we may say that we communicate the gospel by *speaking* it, by *writing* it, and by *living* it, so that other people may *hear* it and *read* it and *see* it. Luke the evangelist provides an admirable illustration of this. He did the work of an evangelist in each of these three ways.

1. *Luke wrote the good news*

When we speak of Luke as the evangelist we mean that he was the author of the written gospel that bears his name. We should remember that he was also the author of The Acts, which is the sequel to the gospel and continues the story of the beginnings of Christianity. Between them these two books represent about a quarter of the entire New Testament, and that fact alone reminds us of how much we owe to him.

It is not really surprising that Luke occupies so important a place among the New Testament writers. For not only was he, as a physician, a cultured and highly educated man; he also, as a Greek, belonged to a literary-minded people. It is generally agreed that Luke was a fine scholar, a first-rate historian, and a master of the Greek language. So, not unnaturally, when he became a Christian he decided he must use his gifts to write the story of Jesus Christ. Other attempts had already been made to do this, as he acknowledges in the preface to his gospel (Luke 1.1–4); but none of those he had seen struck him as altogether satisfactory and for that reason he set about compiling a record which was accurate, trustworthy and orderly.

The result of Luke's putting pen to paper (or rather to papyrus, the sort of paper used in those days) is that we now have in our New Testament a matchless portrait of the Lord Jesus as the Son of Man and the Saviour of the world. Here, more clearly than in any of the other gospels, we see our Lord in all the perfection and beauty of his manhood, manifesting through his life and teaching the redeeming grace of God to lost humanity.

Luke certainly did the work of an evangelist by what he wrote. The same is true of a multitude of dedicated Christian writers since his day. Literature has all along played a vitally important part in the story of Christianity and in the work of evangelism; and never was its role more significant that in our own day when, with the spread of world literacy, a vast new reading public has been brought within reach of the written word. Hence the call to us as Christians to 'feed the minds of millions' with the truth of God through the various literature agencies and the Bible societies. Luke we may say was a pioneer in all this. Hundreds of years ago he helped to spread the good news by means of his pen.

2. *Luke was a missionary preacher*

But more. Luke was not only a gospel writer. He was also a gospel preacher. Admittedly we do not know a great deal about this aspect of his life and work, but we do know that he accompanied Paul on several of his journeys through the Roman empire. There are passages of the Acts—the so-called 'we' passages—where Luke writes in the first personal plural, making clear that at these points in the narrative he himself was a member of the missionary party.

Why did he join the party? He went with Paul, surely, not simply as a friend to keep him company or as a doctor to minister to his health but as a whole-hearted partner in the task of evangelism. That is why Paul describes him in his letter to Philemon as one of his 'fellow-workers'—that is, as one who laboured with him in the service of the gospel.

Luke as we know was a man greatly in love with the gospel. As he travelled from place to place he must have revelled in every opportunity of telling the story of Christ to others. Tradition connects his name in particular with Antioch in Syria, which became the leading centre of Christian missionary enterprise. From the Acts story it would seem that Luke was left in charge of the newly formed church at Philippi and here doubtless he exercised an effective ministry as evangelist, pastor and teacher. At any rate, we know from Paul's letter to the Philippians, written some ten years later, that a strong Christian community was built up in that Macedonian city. Was the church at Philippi itself a witness to Luke's missionary labours and preaching?

3. *Luke practised the gospel*

I use the word practised deliberately and give it a double meaning. For Luke was a medical practitioner ('dear doctor Luke' is what Paul calls him in Colossians) and in exercising the ministry of healing he was in a true sense practising the gospel. He was revealing the love of Christ to men in deed and not merely in word.

It is sometimes said that Luke was the first medical missionary. But surely not the *first*. I am reminded of the words of Dr David Livingstone who declared that God had only one Son and he made him a medical missionary. If our Lord was the first medical missionary we may certainly claim that Luke the beloved physician followed closely in his steps. Like his Master he too went about doing good, healing the sick and binding up the wounds of suffering humanity. His life reminds us that the preaching of the good news is all of a piece with the service of mankind.

Luke was in many ways the complete evangelist. We may sum up his work by saying that he penned the gospel, he preached the gospel, and he practised the gospel. To us in our day there comes the call to do the work of an evangelist, that is, to communicate the good news; and, like Luke, we can do that by writing it for others to read, speaking it for others to hear, and living it for others to see.

ST SIMON AND ST JUDE

The Zealot

Luke 6.15 '*Simon who was called the Zealot.*'

The two men whom the Church commemorates today both bear apostolic names which are thoroughly familiar to us all though the men themselves are practically unknown. This anomaly is accounted for by the fact that there were among our Lord's apostles *two* men called Simon and *two* called Judas (just as there were also two men who bore the name of James). The Simon we all know is the Simon to whom Jesus gave the name of Peter, the Rock man, and the Judas who has gained notoriety is the one known as Iscariot, the man of Kerioth, who turned traitor. Today we are concerned with neither of these but with the other Simon and the other Judas.

What do we know about them? Very little indeed. In fact about the other Judas we really know nothing except that he was also called Thaddaeus and that he asked Jesus a question at the last supper (John 14.22). However, we can glean something about 'Simon who was called the Zealot' and I invite you to think about him for a few minutes.

1. *Simon the freedom fighter*

The fact that this man was called *Zelotes* almost certainly indicates that before he became a disciple of Jesus he had been a member of the Jewish party known as the Zealots. They were a band of fanatical nationalists whose aim was the liberation of Israel from the dominion of Rome and whose methods were those of violence and armed revolt. The more extreme members bore the name of the Assassins. They were the sort of freedom fighters of their day. They were certainly not unlike the I.R.A. in the Ireland of our own time. Josephus the Jewish historian described them as men with 'an inviolable attachment to liberty', who claimed that God alone was their Ruler and Lord and who were prepared to endure any sort of suffering to free the chosen people from their hated foreign overlords.

However mistaken they were in their ideas and ways, the Zealots were undoubtedly men of heroic and reckless courage who, true to their name, were fired with an unquenchable zeal for the sanctity of the Jewish law and the emancipation of the Jewish people.

It is against this sort of background that we must try to understand Simon the Zealot. How he became a disciple of Jesus we do not know and in any case it doesn't matter very much. But *why* did he become a disciple? That's the important question. What did this bold and fervent patriot expect to find in Jesus? Almost certainly he thought of him in terms of the promised Son of David. He hoped that Jesus would be a mighty warrior king who would free his people from the Roman tyranny, set up his throne in Jerusalem and establish God's kingdom in power and glory among the nations.

Such in all probability were the expectations of this man. How far were those expectations realised? What did he in fact find in Jesus? And why did Jesus eventually choose him as one of the twelve?

2. *Christ the emancipator*

I think we may say that Simon's expectations were at once disappointed and fulfilled when he joined the company of the disciples. I have a feeling that he was considerably puzzled at first. Certainly before long he must have been compelled to rethink many of his basic assumptions and ideals.

(1) For one thing, Jesus was a different sort of Messiah from what Simon had expected, a different kind of liberator. True enough, he was indeed the Lord's anointed King, the promised redeemer of Israel, the inaugurator of the heavenly kingdom. To this extent Simon's hopes were fully realised. But, as he was soon to discover, Jesus had come to rescue men from the tyranny of sin, not from the bondage of Rome. He had come to establish a kingdom of grace, not a worldly empire. He had come to reign in men's hearts and lives, not on a glittering throne. And furthermore, his redeeming purpose was to be accomplished not by force of arms but by way of the cross;

for his own life blood was the price he had to pay for the ransom of men's souls.

(2) Again, Simon discovered that Jesus' methods and motives were quite different from those he had been accustomed to. The Zealot's way was that of violence and hatred. Christ's way was that of love and self-sacrifice. Dr William Barclay has described Simon the Zealot as the man who began by hating and ended by loving. It was Jesus who drove the hatred from his heart and taught him to love. No doubt Simon came to see in course of time that he had been fighting before for the wrong sort of freedom and that the weapons of the world cannot advance the kingdom of God.

(3) But this too we may be sure Simon came to see: that Christ and his cause demanded from him quite as much burning enthusiasm as he had displayed before as a member of the Zealot party. I like to think that when he enlisted in the service of his new Master he did not lose his old zest. I believe the Lord must have welcomed into the ranks of his disciples a man of such passionate devotion. Indeed it may be that this is the reason why the Lord appointed him as one of the twelve: not because he was a man of outstanding gifts or brilliant accomplishments (probably he was not) but because he was a man with a burning heart who encouraged others by his love and zeal and courage.

3. *Christian zealots today*

Do we not need today more people of this kind? Where are the Christian zealots in our churches?

Christ has no place in his service for luke-warm Christians, as the story of the Church of the Laodiceans reminds us (Revelation 3.15f.). No wonder the cause of Christ languishes when hearts are cold and Christians become worldly and complacent and self-satisfied! That is what was wrong at Laodicea.

What about ourselves? Are we zealots for Christ? Do our hearts burn with enthusiasm for the furtherance of God's kingdom in the world? Perhaps we have lost the fire we once had. Perhaps the flame of our devotion needs to be rekindled. If so, then we must pray with Charles Wesley:

O thou who camest from above,
The pure celestial fire to impart,
Kindle a flame of sacred love
On the mean altar of my heart.

There let it for thy glory burn
With inextinguishable blaze,
And trembling to its source return
In humble prayer, and fervent praise.

ALL SAINTS' DAY

The quality of sainthood

Matthew 5.1, 2 '*Seeing the crowds, Jesus went up on the mountain, and when he sat down his disciples came to him. And he opened his mouth and taught them.*'

Beyond question the most famous sermon ever preached was the Sermon on the Mount. The preacher was the Lord Jesus himself and he began his sermon with what we have come to call the beatitudes. It is those beatitudes which form the gospel appointed for the feast of All Saints. I would invite you to look at them now and see how they delineate a character, suggest a contrast, and present a challenge.

1. *A character*

In the first place the beatitudes delineate a *character*: the character of true saintliness. It is this that makes them so wholly appropriate to form today's gospel.

I think it is important that we should be clear that the beatitudes have to do primarily with character rather than with conduct. Not that conduct is unimportant—by no means. But conduct is determined by character and in the end it is what we *are* that matters most of all.

Here then we have Christ's own picture of saintliness, the character of those who receive the blessing of the Lord. This, I believe, is the way we should understand the word *blessed* at the beginning of each of these short sentences. Some modern versions render it 'happy' or even 'fortunate', but Jesus is not talking here about human happiness or good fortune. He is speaking about the kind of people who inherit God's blessing. The NEB hits the nail on the head with its rendering 'How blest are those . . .'.

Who are the people God blesses? Here is the list as Jesus gives it in this sermon. First, the 'poor in spirit'—that is, those who are deeply aware of their spiritual poverty and who cast themselves wholly on the grace of God and so enter the heavenly kingdom. Next, those who 'mourn': those who sorrow for sin (their own and that of the world) and who grieve to see God's cause languishing. Then there are the 'meek', a word which indicates the quality of submissiveness: the readiness to yield in all things to the Lord and to others for his sake. Those who 'hunger and thirst for righteousness' are the people who long and labour to see right prevail, evil overthrown, and the will of God triumphant. The 'merciful' are in a special sense those who render service to the poor and needy and exhibit a forgiving spirit. The 'pure in heart' are people who are clean *inside*. Jesus is stressing that ritual purity is not enough. The heart must be clean in God's sight. So we come to the seventh beatitude, 'How blest are the peacemakers'. The peacemakers are those who exercise a ministry of reconciliation in every sphere of life where there is division and strife.

2. *A contrast*

Such is the quality of true saintliness. Now clearly the kind of character depicted here stands in stark contrast to the character of the typical 'man of the world'. Christ's pattern of discipleship and the world's standards and ideals are two very different things. We are thinking now of the 'world', of course, in the biblical sense, as human society organised apart from God.

The world does not pronounce any blessing on those who know themselves to be spiritually poor. It blesses the proud and the self-sufficient. The world does not mourn for sin; it mocks at sin. The world has no use for the meek; it glorifies the mighty. It hungers not for righteousness but for wealth, success, fame, pleasure. It does not follow the line of mercy; it advocates toughness. It is not concerned with purity of heart but simply with keeping up appearances. It despises the peacemakers and exalts the war-mongers.

So the beatitudes suggest a contrast—and a conflict. That's why Jesus added an eighth beatitude: 'Blessed are those who are persecuted for righteousness' sake, for theirs is the kingdom of heaven.' The final beatitude is even more personal and pointed: 'Blessed are *you* when men revile you and persecute and utter all kinds of evil against you falsely on my account.' Jesus knew full well that the saintly character he described—and which he himself exemplified—would not win the world's admiration but rather the world's animosity. For him it meant the cross. Many of his saints down the centuries, and especially those who have been most like him, have suffered the same sort of fate. The martyr-Church in our own day—for example, in lands behind the iron curtain—tells the same story. It's not really popular to be a saint.

3. *A challenge*

What about ourselves? Do not the beatitudes present a challenge to us who are also 'called to be saints'? And the challenge is this: first, to examine our own hearts and to see quite honestly how far we come short of the pattern our Lord presents to us. Secondly, to cultivate the qualities which make for Christian saintliness and to know the blessedness which accompanies it. And thirdly, to be ready to face the world's scorn and opposition and to follow God's saints in the path of suffering.

It's not an easy path, and mercifully we are not all called

upon to tread it. But when the call does come the words of our Lord at the end of today's Gospel are a tremendous encouragement: 'Rejoice and be glad, for your reward is great in heaven, for so men persecuted the prophets who were before you.'

> And when the strife is fierce, the warfare long,
> Steals on the ear the distant triumph-song,
> And hearts are brave again and arms are strong.
> Alleluia!

(W. Walsham How)